THE MUSIC OF THE BEATLES

THE MUSIC
OF
THE BEATLES

TWILIGHT OF THE GODS

Wilfrid Mellers

Schirmer Books
A Division of Macmillan Publishing Co., Inc.
NEW YORK

Published by arrangement with THE VIKING PRESS,
INC.

First Paperback Printing 1975

SCHIRMER BOOKS
A Division of Macmillan Publishing Co., Inc.
866 Third Avenue, New York, N.Y. 10022

SBN 670-73598-1

Library of Congress catalog card number: 73-3508

Printed in U.S.A.

To Judy and Caroline
'but for whom,' etc.

Contents

Acknowledgements

The publishers would like to express their gratitude to Northern Songs Limited for permission to quote extracts from the following songs* (all songs copyright Northern Songs Ltd. for the world):

I saw her standing there	© 1963
All I've got to do	1963
Misery	1963
Do you want to know a secret	1963
It won't be long	1963
Hold me tight	1963
A hard day's night	1964
If I fell	1964
Any time at all	1964
Things we said today	1964
You can't do that	1964
I'll follow the sun	1964
You're going to lose that girl	1965
You've got to hide your love away	1965
Yesterday	1965
Drive my car	1965
Norwegian wood	1965
Girl	1965
Michelle	1965
Wait	1965
The word	1965
Taxman (Harrison)	1966
Eleanor Rigby	1966
I'm only sleeping	1966
Here there and everywhere	1966
Good day sunshine	1966

* All songs by Lennon and McCartney unless otherwise stated.

For no one	1966
Got to get you into my life	1966
Tomorrow never knows	1966
Penny Lane	1967
Strawberry fields forever	1967
Sergeant Pepper's lonely hearts club band	1967
Lucy in the sky with diamonds	1967
Fixing a hole	1967
She's leaving home	1967
Within you without you (Harrison)	1967
When I'm sixty-four	1967
A day in the life	1967
All you need is love	1967
Your mother should know	1967
The fool on the hill	1967
I am the walrus	1967
Blue jay way (Harrison)	1967
Blackbird	1968
Honey Pie	1968
Dear Prudence	1968
I'm so tired	1968
Sexy Sadie	1968
Julia	1968
Goodnight	1968
Across the universe	1968
Come together	1969
O darling	1969
I want you (she's so heavy)	1969
Because	1969
You never give me your money	1969
Golden slumbers	1969
Yer Blues	1969
The long and winding road	1970
That would be something (McCartney)	1970
Maybe I'm amazed (McCartney)	1970
Teddy boy (McCartney)	1970
Mother (Lennon)	1970

Hold on (Lennon) 1970
I found out (Lennon) 1970
Isolation (Lennon) 1970
Remember (Lennon) 1970
Well, well, well (Lennon) 1970
Look at me (Lennon) 1970
Long haired lady (Paul and Linda McCartney) 1971
Imagine (Lennon) 1971
Jealous Guy (Lennon) 1971
It's so hard 1971
I don't wanna be a soldier (Lennon) 1971
Oh my love (Lennon-Ono) 1971
How do you sleep (Lennon) 1971
How (Lennon) 1971

Note to the American Reader

Because of the considerable difference between British and American terms for rhythmic values, we are including the following table for the convenience of the American reader.

	British	American
𝅝	semibreve	whole note
𝅗𝅥	minim	half note
♩	crotchet	quarter note
♪	quaver	eighth note
𝅘𝅥𝅯	semiquaver	sixteenth note

There are also differences between British and American versions of some Beatle albums. *With the Beatles*, for example, was released in the United States as *Meet the Beatles*. The American version of *Rubber Soul* does not include *Drive my car* and *Nowhere man*, discussed here, and includes other songs not discussed. The British versions are referred to throughout.

Preface

This book, being about Beatle music, includes a fair proportion of analytical commentary, since descriptive accounts of music cannot be valid unless they are based on what happens in musical terms. After some hesitation, I've decided to incorporate quotations of the music because this makes for easier reading: in a small sea of technicalities the eye from time to time welcomes something to latch on to. Yet music quotation, even in reference to literate 'art' music, can never be adequate; in reference to Beatle music (and to most pop, jazz, folk and non-Western music) it may be not only inadequate but also misleading: for written notation can represent neither the improvised elements nor the immediate distortions of pitch and flexibilities of rhythm which are the essence (not a decoration) of a music orally and aurally conceived. It follows that my commentary can be fully intelligible only in relationship to the sound of the music; the book should be a 'companion' to the playing of the discs. If scores of the songs are available also, so much the better, so long as one realises that the notated scores are only an approximation to the sounds produced. In early Beatle songs the approximation of the published scores to the actual sounds is very crude. In later songs some attempt seems to have been made to write down what is heard, in so far as this is possible within the limitations of musical literacy. The ultimate arbiter is one's ears.

Some people seem to find it inherently risible that pop music should be discussed in technical terms at all; when the senior critic of *The Times* wrote the first musically literate piece about the Beatles it was greeted with hoots of mirth both from the Beatles themselves and from their hostile critics. This is curious, for there is no valid way of talking about the experiential 'effects' of music except by starting from an account of what actually happens in musical technique, the terminology for which has been evolved by professional musicians over some centuries. The fact that a Beatle – or a jazzman or a peasant singer or a perhaps highly sophisticated oriental musician – has never heard of a dominant seventh or a mediant relationship or whatever, is neither here nor there; people who live and work in 'oral' traditions have no need critically to rationalise about what they are doing. Of course it is possible to argue that all discussion of and writing about music is a waste of time; I've occasionally come near to saying this myself. However, if this is true, it applies to all discussion of all music equally: analysis of Beethoven is no less irrelevant than analysis of Beatles. If one is to attempt analysis of either – and obviously on balance I think it is both possible and worth while to do so – one has no choice but to start from the musical facts; and has no means of describing them except in the accepted terminology.

In Beatle music the musical facts are not, compared with those in Beethoven's music, very complicated, though they may be of some subtlety, partly because they are not entirely literate. The number of terms needed for reference is modest; and I have appended a glossary which attempts to describe the *aural effect* of the particular technical process. Any reader who is prepared to devote a little time to the glossary should be able to read the book, I hope with profit, whether or no he can comprehend normal staff notation. Some familiarity with guitar figuration will be a help, of course; it is not true that pop musicians never talk in technicalities, though their terminology is not identical with that of the 'straight' musician.

I have confined my attention to songs on the extant LPs. This doesn't cover the Beatles' musical career comprehensively, but is adequately representative; there seemed little point in discussing songs unless one has ready access to the recorded sound. Since the purpose of the book is understanding rather than evaluation, I've commented mostly on songs which I believe to be good; obviously the better songs are the more revealing. It doesn't follow that there are no inferior Beatle songs; none the less the proportion of good songs to bad is remarkably high. This is a cheering note to end a preface on. Numerically and commercially, the Beatles were the most successful of rock-pop musicians;

artistically, they were also the best. This should afford some comfort if, reviewing man's story in the second half of the twentieth century, one feels tempted, by his apparently ineradicable folly, to despair.

The book started as a series of open lectures which I was invited to give in the University of York. I acknowledge a general debt to the University, and a specific one to the many young people who attended the lectures and, in discussion afterwards, offered comment, criticism and some basic information I'd otherwise have missed. In particular I must thank Geoffrey Pullum, of the University's Department of Language, for reading the MS and noting discrepancies and errors. Most of the corrections made by him and other young readers have been incorporated in the text: though I eventually gave up any attempt at an 'authoritative' interpretation of Beatle texts since the 'in'-interpretations are mutually contradictory. This applies both to the words of Beatle lyrics and to their verbal pronouncements about their Life and Work; the latter, of course, were sometimes deliberately meant to mislead. This is not important, since the Beatles' twentieth-century mythology – which is why they matter – is incarnate in their songs as artefacts: which he who runs may read, so long as he doesn't allow the irrelevancies to blind (and deafen) him.

Department of Music　　　　　　　　　　　　　W. M.
University of York
December 1971

'Many people ask what are Beatles? Why
Beatles? Ugh, Beatles! How did the name
arrive? So we will tell you. It came in a vision.
A man appeared on a flaming pie and said unto
them, From this day on you are Beatles with
an A. Thank you, Mister Man, they said,
thanking him.
   And so they were Beatles.'

John Lennon 1960

'Just come back in twenty years' time and see
what we're doing, and who's doing what.
Don't put me – don't sort of mark my papers
like I'm top of the maths class or did I come in
Number One in English Language because I
never did. Just assess me on what I am and
what comes out of me mouth, and what me
work is. Don't mark me in classrooms. It's like
I've just left school again! I just graduated
from the school of show biz or whatever it
was called.'

John Lennon 1970

Part One
Novice's
Departure

1. Prologue and Initiation

Elgar must be the last composer whose music as a private testament is, if different from, inseparably related to, his work as a public statement; perhaps it is fortuitous that he virtually relinquished composition around 1914, the year that initiated the Great Wars that may mark the beginning of the end of 'Western' civilisation. However this may be, most composers since 1914 have found themselves asking questions to which there is no comfortable answer: precisely what function(s) has the composer in the modern world? why does he spend so much time on so difficult an occupation, in most cases with so little material reward and so little evidence that other people, apart from a cluster of (usually prejudiced) composers and a shrivel of critics, have much interest in sharing this experience? Thirty or forty years ago our lonely 'art' composer would have recognised that there was another branch of the musical profession wherein he could make money and attract a sizeable audience: but would have rejected this popular field on the grounds that, in pandering to the baser instincts for escape and entertainment, it denied the artist's birthright – which was to make people more, not less, aware of pain, anguish, ecstasy, etc., as experienced by a human being (meaning me) endowed with a more than average quota of sensitivity. Today, our composer finds his position more equivocal. Though he may still regard much of today's pop music as a commercialised industry, he can hardly deny that pop now embraces music that cannot be described as entertainment, let alone evasion. For better and/or worse, this music is also a way of life; and it is precisely some such sense of commitment that our 'art' composer misses in his own relationship to a public. To a large number of young people pop music seems passionately to *matter*. While it does not, except in some rather dubious senses, make us more 'aware', it is not an embellishment of living which one can take or leave; it *does something*, being 'music of necessity'

in somewhat the same sense as this phrase is applied to the
musics of primitive peoples. So our composer finds himself
asking further questions: what is it that pop music does that my
music does not? *what* necessity does it commit one to? how valid
is the parallel between the 'rituals' of pop and those of genuinely
primitive cultures?

To begin with, we must establish what is meant by this phrase,
music of necessity; and may profitably start from the observation
of our own childhood. When little girls sing and dance 'Wallflowers, wallflowers, growing up so high' they are enacting a rite
which unconsciously prepares them for the fact of mortality: (1)*
just as other sung and danced games initiate them into the
mysteries of puberty, courtship and marriage. For even in our
modern industrial communities children's games effect – over and
above their entertainment value as an explosion of animal
spirits – a temporary suspension of normal life for the sacred
session of play. They take place within strict boundaries of time
and place (the magic line or circle), usually with disguise
('dressing up') to separate the in-group from the common world;
and they involve an element of ordered body movement (dance),
usually accompanied by musical melody (song), sometimes without
words, sometimes with nonsense words, sometimes with verbal
language that is meaningful 'below' the level of consciousness.
Such basic play-rituals are hardly distinguishable from those of
primitive peoples, who have no word to denote art, since living
through their myths in dance and song is the essence, not an
extension, of their lives: if the myths are not enacted, breath may
cease, the sun be obliterated, the moon no longer control the
tides. Myth must be projected into body movements and into
sound: which may or may not involve language; which may or may
not be reinforced by instruments that are not mere noise-producers
but also extensions of the human body, symbols of human
attributes (female and womb-like in the case of drums, male and
phallic in the case of flutes).

Thus, at the most rudimentary level, there is a game played by

* In this chapter the numbers are record references, listed in
discography on pages 208–9.

Eskimo children who, taking the tubs used by their parents for storing whale oil, blow into them rhythmically (2). Whilst this activity would seem to begin fortuitously, the children soon explore pattern-making, variations of stress and timbre; and it is impossible to say at what point a game shades into an act of profound ritual significance. All the time, the Eskimos believe, God is pouring out life into animate nature; what would happen if, one day, he had no puff left? So humbly we pay back to God our tribute of the breath of life, which is the ultimate mystery. Another very primitive people, the Australian aborigine, makes a music consisting of isolated words and phrases – invocations of sun, moon, cloud and other natural phenomenon – yelled against the everlasting drone of the dijiridu and accompanied by the rhythmic beating of sticks (3). In the silent emptiness the aborigine dramatises the basic fact of his life: the beating of the pulse, the thudding of the heart. A third primitive people, the African bushmen who live in the Kalahari desert, create a fascinating music by emulating the squeaks and squawks of birds, the growls and grunts of beasts (4). In becoming, in sound and movement, their totemic creatures, they employ disguise and illusion as a propitiatory act, conquering fear of the unknown in paying reverence to the creatures on whom they depend for subsistence.

At a more sophisticated level totem music and dance become an act, not of propitiation, but of affirmation. For the South Plains Indians the horse is a beast wild but not unknowable; so, affirming his and their phallic dominance, they may sing 'tumbling strains' which, beginning on a high note, descend savagely to create an effect of uncontrolled libido, sustained by the drums' or rattles' remorseless beat (5).

The Indians' horse songs are wordless, or such language as they have is nonsensical or magical. Yet the word too emerged in the dark backward of Time: as when the Maori shaman clasps in his arms the tree on which his people rely for food, clothing, shelter and transport, and talks to it in a strange, ululatory chant halfway between speech and song (6). If he creates melody, it is at most a two-tone incantation; yet it entails the basic elements of music as ritual – repetition, order, rhythmic alteration, inducing

rapture and trance. Much the same is true of the negative aspects
of primitive ritual, such as Haitian voodoo (7). In invoking
demons, the celebrant risks being possessed by them, as he must
be in more positive terms by his gods or totemic creatures.
Possession may be also exorcism; and 'talking in tongues', to the
pounding drum and clanging bell, is an expiatory act, whether it
be with Haitian voodooists, or with West Indian Pentecostalists
living in London today. Paradoxically, the Pentecostalists recognise
the gift of tongues by 'the totally inarticulate gabbling of Alleluyas'
(Mary Douglas). 'The more he is inarticulate, the more proof that
the speaker is unconscious and not in control of what is being
imparted to him. Inarticulateness is taken as evidence of divine
inspiration. So also are "dancing in the Spirit", involuntary
twirling and prancing, and involuntary twitching and shuddering
taken to be a sign of blessing.'

Music of necessity went underground with 'Western' civilisation's growing awareness of consciousness, which was first
supremely exemplified in, and bequeathed to Christian Europe
by, the Greeks. None the less shamanistic rites were among the
seminal sources of Greek tragedy as well as comedy, and survived
through the centuries in the plough cycles, sword dances and epic
laments of European peasant societies; even in the civilised
hey-day of the Renaissance they are present, tamed into sophisticated artefacts, in the Green Men and satyrs of the court masque.
In our twentieth-century industrial society jazz sprang from a
tension between black melody, modality and rhythm and white
harmony and metre; and as late as 1936 a 'primitive' blues singer
such as Robert Johnson gives a scarily neurotic intensity to age-old
techniques of pitch distortion and rhythmic ellipsis, creating in
Hellhound on my Trail a music dedicated to demonic possession (8).
This, of course, is the alienated frenzy of the black Outsider;
would it, however, be true to say that the (largely white) pop
explosion that occurred in the wake of the Second World War is
also a rediscovery of music as orgiastic magic, now relevant, in its
caprine potency, not merely to a black minority, but to the young
at large, over most of our globally scattered, electronically pro-
cessed technocracy?

In the early fifties Elvis the Pelvis, Bill Haley, Chuck Berry and others offered a streamlined mechanisation of black blues and barrelhouse music interfused with white Country Western, and the British Beatles achieved their earliest and most lunatically hysterical successes with such rocking and rolling numbers. They scored a colossal hit with Chuck Berry's *Roll over Beethoven* (9) – the very title of which is a rejection of Western civilisation! And they were second to none in attaining orgiastic frenzy as they *Twist and Shout* (10). Between such music and our primitive musics of necessity there are certain obvious parallels.

First, in the rock and roll explosion which initiated the new pop after the Second World War the word, with intellectually communicable meaning, is almost totally insignificant. 'Men sang out their feelings,' says the linguist Jesperson, 'long before they were able to speak their thoughts'; and for Elvis Presley, Chuck Berry and the early Beatles, language was not a natural adjustment of ways to means but, as Susanne K. Langer has put it, a 'purposeless lulling instinct', a trigger for magical release. The solo singers in modern folk tradition, as distinct from rock and beat groups, are of course an exception to this, for since the words carried a social and even political message it was important that they should be heard. Yet it is interesting that the evolution of Bob Dylan's songs moves from overt protest into the archetypal imagery and incremental rhythms of folk poetry, and into surrealistic techniques of free association. Indeed the verses of all his songs – and those of a Leonard Cohen, a Joni Mitchell, a Sandy Denny – re-create oral rather than literate principles of composition; like real folk poetry and children's runes they live in mythological rather than in chronological Time, and have little use for intellectually comprehensible sequence.

Secondly, the nature of the tunes (both of folk soloists and of rock groups) is conditioned by their origins in the most primitive forms of the Negro blues, in the monody of the 'poor white' American, and in American Indian, Mexican and European folk sources. This means that the melodies tend to be pentatonic, or at most modally heptatonic: and are so not – at least initially – by deliberate imitation but because such are the formulae (minimal, alienated, dispossessed) from which song germinates.

Thirdly, these tunes are performed with varied techniques of vocal production, with distortions of pitch and elongations and ellipses of rhythm which are un-notatable in terms of conventional musical literacy, but relatable to folk and primitive origins: consider Otis Redding's African-cum-Gospel shout, Dylan's poor-white croak, Mick Jagger's African-cum-American-Indian yelling, the Beatles' broad Liverpudlianism. The wordless refrains are vocalised regression, emulating the cry of the newborn babe (which may also be the chuckle or hum of the deity), attempting to re-enact the primal relationship of mother and child.

Fourthly, instrumental sonorities also derive from these rudimentary sources, electric guitars and organs being vastly amplified permutations of blues guitar, country banjo, harmonica, bagpipes and so on. The amplification, in more recent pop, tends to intensify the primitivism, because electronics may create a nightmarish inflation of the pitch distortions expressively endemic to folk music.

Fifthly, whereas in the pop music of the previous generation harmony – a European phenomenon associated with awareness of duality – may be of some sophistication, in today's pop it is, complementary to the melodic characteristics mentioned above, rudimentary or non-existent. The nostalgic chromatics of a Jerome Kern, the cynically witty harmonic surprises of a Cole Porter, give way to primitive drones and ostinati. Even the wide-eyed, open-eared effects created in Beatle songs by mediant relationships and side-stepping modulations are the empirical product of the movement of melody, modally conceived, and of the behaviour of the hands on guitar strings or keyboard. Similar accidents occur in medieval and early Renaissance music, with a comparable synthesis of innocence with sophistication.

Sixthly, since pop music is made by ear-musicians, not eye-musicians, it resembles folk and primitive musics in involving improvisation, variations on simple patterns within clearly defined but unnotated conventions. The musical illiteracy of some pop performers is thus as irrelevant as is the illiteracy of jazzmen:

though the contact of Negro jazz with its primitive (African) sources is more direct, less subject to commercial pressures.

Seventhly (especially in the group-music), the incremental repetition of brief, non-developing phrases, with or without intelligible words, generates and at the same time is generated by an unremittent beat. The continuity of the beat destroys the sense of temporal progression, so that one lives once more in mythological, rather than in chronological, Time. The trance the music induces may be enhanced by narcotics: as was certainly the case in primitive music rituals, and probably in those of the Greeks, Minoans, Cretans, and the great oriental cultures.

Our seventh point has effected the crucial transition from pop as music to pop as dance · to which the concept of the Group is itself pertinent. For whereas the modern folk soloist such as Dylan is essentially a loner, the group seeks corporate identity. From Elvis to early Beatles' rock and beat achieved a commercially exploitable form of Negroid blues and stomp, with white Country and Western music thrown in as ballast; and the music's corporeal energy promoted action whereby the young found the Nirvana that Wagner's Tristan, after several hundred years of 'consciousness', had been seeking, literally knocking themselves senseless as well as mindless. The dancing was not couple dancing, which implies a two-way love relationship; jerking alone, the individual dancer rather resembled the dervish who simultaneously asserts his body and seeks release, against the law of gravity, from the inertia of matter, becoming a human structure that (as Heinrich von Kleist has told us in his famous essay, 'Uber das Marionettentheater') either has 'no consciousness at all or an infinite one – that is, a puppet, or God'.

The loss of identity in a communal act is reinforced both by drugs and by the quality of the sound, which is itself narcotic. The Negroid voice, simulated by white men, substituted aggression for nervosity, and instrumental resources followed suit. Percussion was more violent than authentic primitive drumming, both because it was metrically cruder and because, in amplification, it was so loud. Similarly, whereas the Negro's guitar was often savage but sometimes, like his voice, intimately expressive, and whereas the white man's country guitar or banjo was cheery if insensitive, pop's vastly amplified electric guitars and organs became a plangent resonance that engulfs consciousness; the electronic fuzzbuzz effect is extraordinarily close to the raucous resonance favoured by many African peoples, and it is improbable that this occurred through conscious emulation. In primitive musics demonic possession denies 'personal' expression; in modern rock the immense sea of sound has a comparable effect, on a vaster scale, and loudness becomes paradoxically more silent than silence, since one is no longer aware of gradation.

Yet if this is broadly true of 'mechanised' commerical rock, it isn't the whole truth about the Beatles, even in their early days; certainly it doesn't adequately account for the phenomenal success of their own songs as compared with those taken over from rock tradition. What, we have now to ask, did the Beatles themselves bring to the rock experience?

Partly, of course, it was a matter of their Merseyside background. John, looking back at his boyhood from 1970, has spoken precisely and poetically of the meaning of Liverpool for adolescent Beatles:

'It was a port. That means it was less hick than somewhere in the English Midlands, like the American Midwest or whatever you call it. We were a port, the second biggest port in England, between Manchester and London. The North was where the money was made in the Eighteen Hundreds, that was where the brass and all the heavy people were, and that's where the despised people were. We were the ones that were looked down upon as animals by the Southerners, the Londoners . . . We were a great amount of Irish descent, and blacks and Chinamen, all sorts there. It was like San Fransisco . . .

There was nothing big in Liverpool; it wasn't American. It was going poor, a very poor city, and tough. But people have a sense of humour because they are in so much pain, so they are always cracking jokes. They are very witty and it's an Irish place. It's where the Irish came when they ran out of potatoes, and it's where the black people were left or worked as slaves or whatever. It is cosmopolitan, and it's where the sailors would come home with the blues records from America on the ships. There is the biggest Country and Western following in England in Liverpool, besides London, always besides London, because there is more of it there.

I heard Country and Western music in Liverpool before I heard rock and roll. The people there – the Irish in Ireland are the same – take their Country and Western music very seriously . . . There were established folk, blues and Country and Western clubs in Liverpool before rock and roll and we were like the new kids coming out. I remember the first guitar I ever saw. It belonged to a guy in a cowboy suit in a province in Liverpool, with stars, and a cowboy hat, and a big dobro. They were real cowboys and they took it seriously.'

So the local, the American and the cosmopolitan are inextricably intertwined; though Little Richard and Chuck Berry (who survive as minor heroes among the debris of John's past) may have been the Beatles' initial inspiration, they were formed too by the singing games and runes still acted out by school children in Liverpool streets (11). In such eructations of popular culture one can scarcely disentangle traditional folk sources from music-hall ditties tipsily bellowed in pubs (12) or from dance music blown and scraped by the Celebrated Working Men's Band (13). The fiddle, accordion and cornet, sometimes with string bass as support, sometimes with tin whistle as chirpy obbligato, create a sonority almost as relevant to Beatle music as blues guitar and country harmonica.

Nor, in Liverpool's working-class society, were older, even rural, folk traditions entirely submerged. In Lancashire mining areas austere, old-style modal tunes surprisingly survived (14); in dark dockland pubs one could still hear cheekily irreverent urban recreations of ancient rural songs, such as Frank Harte's version of *Lord Randal*, clipping the modality of the old tune into a cross between music-hall farce and kids' street jingle (15). Irish reels and Scottish jigs abounded; one of the Beatles' earliest successes was a rock version of *My Bonnie lies over the ocean* –

through which number, indeed, they were launched on their international career, since it tickled the fancy of Brian Epstein. Add to these relatively homey musics the musical exotica that sailors of motley racial heritage brought to Liverpool (along with recorded rock and roll), and one sees that the Beatles, in common with other geniuses such as Bach, Mozart and Beethoven, knew the right time and place to be born.

None the less, the time and place won't suffice without the genius, if the word may be used without pretention. So we have now to define the nature of the Beatles' own intuitive contribution: what kind of world did they evoke in their early years, from this interfusion of American black blues and white rock and Country-Western, of Anglo-Irish folk music and song and dance from music-hall and pub? From the start the Beatles were individualities who sought a corporate identity. Though only during the first year or two did Lennon and McCartney actually compose *together*, there's point in the ascription of the songs to their joint authorship. They needed one another for their fulfilment: needed, in a rather different way, the other two Beatles; and the separate ways in which they grew up were affected by the identity they'd sought for in the early years. The interdependence and individuality of the Beatles is a theme we'll be exploring in a later chapter. At this point we need merely to note that their 'group' sense – their corporate identity – is complemented by the themes of the early songs: which concern the euphoric happiness of togetherness, though it's significant that this togetherness is identified with the two-way relationship of heterosexual love – which sometimes becomes synonymous with 'home', security, mum.

One of the most famous of early Beatle songs – *She loves you* – is also quintessential. It is simply an affirmation, epitomised in its 'Yeah yeah yeah' refrain; and it exists in the moment, without before or after. For although its key signature is the E flat beloved of Tin Pan Alley, the opening phrase is pentatonic, or perhaps an aeolian C which veers towards E flat; and although some of the effect depends on contrast between upward tending sharp sevenths and the blue flat sevenths of folk tradition, no conflict is generated, and the song has little sense of a beginning, middle and end. The final guitar chord looks like a triad of E flat major with added sixth; yet the melody suggests that C, not E flat, is the root. The timeless, present-affirming modality is instinctive; and the words, if still perfunctorily vacuous, are no longer *merely* magic talismen, abracadabra. They do concern a basic, life-affirming human experience; and the conjunction of the words with the music makes evident that this experience matters because it is true; and is true because – even in the face of the commercial pressures and discords of modern industrial life – the Beatles are, through their music, as though new-born. It's this pristine quality that helps us to understand the potency of their appeal, the relevance of their mythology. The evidence for this is what happens in their early songs: despite the fact that they began in apparent parasitism, consciously imitating not merely Chuck Berry, Bill Haley and Elvis Presley, but 'anyone from Buddy Holly to Lonnie Donegan, from Frankie Laine to Johnny Ray', and passively accepting the conventions of the pop standard – an eight plus repeated eight bar strain, an eight bar middle, a da capo and occasionally a coda.

The basic Beatle song is Edenic: as is manifest on the first LP in *I saw her standing there*, sung by John and Paul, though apparently Paul was the sole composer. Here are the words:

VERSE
Well, she was just seventeen
You know what I mean,
And the way she looked was way beyond compare.
So how could I dance with another?
O when I saw her standing there.

REPEAT
Well, she looked at me
And I, I could see
That before too long I'd fall in love with her.
She wouldn't dance with another
O when I saw her standing there.

MIDDLE
Well my heart went zoom
When I crossed that room
And I held her hand in mine

DA CAPO   *O we danced through the night*
          And we held each other tight
          And before too long I fell in love with her
          Now I'll never dance with another.

          O when I saw her standing there.

   One couldn't claim that these words are oral poetry, in the
sense that Dylan's songs – even the earliest ones – are: though
in the course of time the Beatles 'grew into' oral poetry, largely
by way of Dylan's example. What these verses do have is an
uncanny instinct for the ways in which people of the Beatles'
generation spoke and felt, rather than thought; and they're
prepared to accept their inarticulateness rather than substitute for
it the 'poetic' insincerities – the moon-June clichés – of the previous generation's pop songs. The blundering phrases of 'unedu-
cated' youth (well, like, see, like, yer know what I mean, like)
and the occasional stilted bookish phrase ('beyond compare')
acquire a certain pathos, if not poetry: so that when he tells us
well she was just seventeen, we do indeed know what he means.
And the tune matches the innocence of the words, for it springs
from the very origins of primitive song, using in the first strain
only four tones, tonic, fifth, second (once) and flat seventh.

Ex. 1

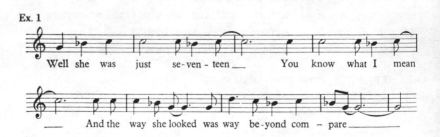

Well she was   just se-ven-teen___ You   know what I   mean

___ And the way she looked was way be-yond com – pare_____

   One couldn't hope for anything more pristine, and the tune
makes her *stand there*, outside Time, teetering between C and
B flat. This is pure folk melody and monody, the flattened

sevenths denying the 'Western' urge to sharpened dominance, aspiration, ambition. The sharp seventh intrudes in the second half of the verse (significantly when he admits the possibility of duality – 'how could I dance with another'); but the verse ends with a timeless pentatonic descent. The middle, when his heart goes zoom, has some harmonic movement and one rudimentary modulation. But there are ten bars instead of sixteen or eight; and the dominant sevenths in B flat are immobilised by repetition, and soon carry us back to a G major dominant and so to the pentatonic tune. The F minor triad on 'Oh' opens the ground beneath our feet, both on its first appearance, and still more in the approach to the final cadence. It's a little revelation, a magic talisman, a 'music of the vowels', as in our primitive examples. We may note too the falsetto (associated by American Indians and other primitives with the supernatural) on the word 'mine' – complementing and counteracting the broad Liverpudlianism.

I've spoken only of the tune (and collaterally of the modality and harmony) in this song; but the effect of the melody is, of course, modified by the rhythm and metre which – as compared with the tune – are fairly complex, with rudimentary African affiliations. The driving rhythm gives to the innocently folk-like tune a certain corporeal energy; and it's this in turn that gives reality to the Edenic dream evoked. Though she may be only seventeen, and we know what he means, the music turns her into a flesh and blood creature also, and makes his embryonic love for real. *All I've got to do* (written and sung by John) is a similar but perhaps subtler case. The ostinato rhythm, though impulsive, is comparatively gentle, and attention is focused on the tender little tune, which is consistently pentatonic and lyrical, and irregular in phrase lengths, five plus two plus four, instead of four plus four. Parallel thirds are used in a way recalling African homophony, as do the vocal melismata. The harmony is restricted to basic triads and the song is entirely without modulation; there is only one passing chromatic, in the approach to the cadence. Literally, in the savages' sense, the song is a love spell: 'All I've gotta do' is call, and she comes; and the final wordless melisma is a magic incantation – a word, incidentally, which derives from the same root as cantare, to sing. The flavour

Ex. 2

Mm

of this adolescent Eden-song is interestingly similar to that of children's dance-songs among certain African peoples, notably the Venda.

Another Eden-song, *Love me do*, written by Paul when he was about sixteen, avoids progression by way of repetition. A two-chord riff remains constant thoughout the first strain, with a three-chord riff in the middle section. The riffs serve as background to a simple tune, Country-American rather than African in flavour, diatonic rather than pentatonic. The child-like, civilisation-purging quality is emphasised by the harmonica-style sonority; and it may be the Country-Western diatonicism that gives this song (as compared with the two previous examples) an air of comic deflation. This becomes explicit in *Misery* (mainly by John) which is about loss – experienced, however, without a whiff of pain. The slightly solemn plagal introduction turns out to be an irony: for it ushers in a G major tune, sung by John and Paul, which is regular in metre and closer to the music-hall than to folk song or blues. The tune – beginning with a falling sixth, then rising up the scale, with an upward pentatonic twist and melisma on *bad* – is guileless, tender yet at the same time perky. The middle section remembers the 'little things' they've done in a *falling scale* and in dorian E minor rather than music-hall G major; but the falling phrase is entirely without harmonic tension and is comically deflated by the piano echo in 'double time' (or in academic terminology, in diminution: see Ex. 3). This is a neat example of how impossible it is to separate words from music in early Beatle songs. The 'misery' refrain mildly mocks the self-pity ('I'm the kind of guy who never used to cry But now you're treating me ba-ha-ha-had, Misery'). Then the instrumental echo

Ex. 3

I re-mem-ber all the lit-tle things we've done

in double time is almost farcical; yet this doesn't finally deflate the lyricism of the first, rising phrase when it returns on the words 'Please come back to me 'cause everyone can see Without you I will be in Misery' (with a capital M at that). The total effect is strangely touching. The humour is self-defensive, for this young thing won't be caught out again; at the same time the longing for togetherness springs from the heart.

Neither *Misery* nor the other songs we have so far commented on contains any explicit reference to the Negro blues which, though it has its own innocence, is riddled with the experience of an ancient, alienated and persecuted race. None the less, blue elements crop up in many early Beatle songs, and without them their later development wouldn't have been possible. *Do you want to know a secret*, written by John for George, has a slow introduction in C minor, with mediant relationships. Because of the modal juxtaposition of plain triads and the painful appoggiatura on 'love you', it sounds rather solemn, certainly serious: which is appropriate enough, since the 'secret' is that he *really*

loves her. When the tune arrives it's happy, but by no means
deflatory in effect, like the tune of *Misery*. For one thing it
breaks the metrical mould of convention, the first strain having
six bars, the second eight, divided as three plus five. Moreover
the tune alternates a rising diatonic scale with chromatically
descending incantations or love-spells; and the intensity hinted at
in the introduction is carried over into the guitar part, which
incorporates chromatic side-steppings suggested by the behaviour
of the hands over the strings. Many guitar clichés of the more

Ex. 4

sophisticated Negro bluesmen are created thus empirically; and
the interior energy of this song grows partly from this relatively
complex if reiterated guitar figuration, partly from the recurrent
false relations between the sharp sevenths in the rising scale
phrase and the flattened fourths of the subdominant (which also
sound like flattened sevenths of C) in the middle section. In the
blues itself false relation was the technical synonym for a clash
between worlds – black melody and monody, white hymn tune

and march. The tension in this song, though it may be latent, is undeniably there, and isn't completely absolved in the conventional I IV V I coda, to which the melody is pure pentatonic ululation: once more a 'pre-conscious' love spell. Significantly it's sung in falsetto, though its range is not high.

This song is still happy and innocent, though less unambiguously Edenic, because more aware of the intensities, if not the agonies, of love. *I wanna be your man* (mainly by Paul) is another, and rather odd, song concerned with the transition between innocence and experience. Technically, it's one of the most primitive, being unadulteratedly pentatonic in melody, with no real modulation, and only two passing chords that might imply tonal movement of any kind. *All* the melodic sevenths are flattened, obsessively hammered at us in the fierce rhythm, denying the (sharp) leading note that implies the 'Western' instinct harmonically to order and control. Yet the nervously driving rhythm, the continuously misplaced vocal accents, imbue the primitivism with frenzy rather than stability: so that paradoxically it turns out to be a song about wanting, yearning, after all: 'I wanna be your man, tell me you understand.' But maybe you don't, and (ouch) maybe I won't make it. There's a hint of desperation in the very will-lessness. The effect of the fade-out is also equivocal. It's not, in this case, because the experience is outside Time, but because we can't (though we'd like to) see an end to it. An Eden is envisaged but we haven't reached it; significantly the piece sounds like a Gospel shout, calling for the promised land. This fierce number is given to Ringo, whose raucous voice rides over his drums that, beating the earth, won't let him take off. His technical deficiencies, as singer, intensify the ferocity; the top notes and false relations are the bluer (and falser) for being out of tune.

There's a subtler effect in *It won't be long*, composed and sung by John, with quasi-African homophony in wordless ululations from the others. The words concern coming home, which means security, mum, as well as the girl; and the power of the song is generated from the tension between awayness and togetherness. The tune begins pentatonically, the dotted rhythm is compulsive and obsessive, as is the fierce descending scale ostinato. But the phrasing is irregular, four plus four, three plus three, four plus four bars; and the modality of the tune generates unstable mediant modulations (C to A flat). The excitement of her return home is

Ex. 5

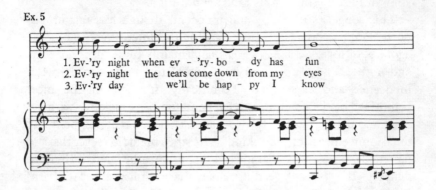

1. Ev-'ry night when ev - 'ry-bo - dy has fun
2. Ev-'ry night the tears come down from my eyes
3. Ev-'ry day we'll be hap - py I know

conveyed by way of a descending chromatic bass, provoking tonal movement: which makes a climax to lead us home on a II V I progression. The ambivalence is reinforced by the pentatonic 'To you', followed by the corny chromatic peroration in the coda. Perhaps the 'African' antiphony between leader and tribe also bears on the awayness-togetherness theme.

Hold me tight, a fairly fierce number mainly by, and lyrically sung by, Paul, has the same ambiguity. It's about never being the Lonely One; and the boy-girl relationship is thus linked to the 'tribal' theme, for the lover is again hardly separable from mum and home. The diatonic tune, with *regularly* pulsing quaver accompaniment, suggests certitude and solidarity, with a whiff of excitement on the syncopated 'tight'. But again this stability is undermined by mediant transitions rather than modulations, these being empirically suggested by the modal tune: whilst the basic instrumental riff – C, F, D 7, G 7, C, C 7, F, F minor – is quite complex. So there's a hint of doubt and unease: being tight, though secure, might also hurt. This is why the cantillating 'ooos' at the end are a punning ambiguity, at once happy and agonised. Musically, they provoke painfully blue false relations between triads of D flat and B flat, sounding simultaneously innocent and vulnerable.

Ex. 6

There's a place, by John, should be mentioned here because it's the first song concerned with *self*-reliance. Despite its melismata and parallel triads, it is curiously austere, resolutely diatonic, virtually without modulation. The 'place' where he thinks of her (again the song, performed by John and Paul, is at once individual and corporate) is his own mind: which is ultimately inviolable, even by her: 'There's a place where I can go When I feel low, When I feel blue, And it's my mind and there's no time When I'm alone.' This is probably the first song wherein we realise that John might be an 'oral' poet, and that in terms of poetic-musical experience he had a long way to travel. Interestingly enough, the melody of the song is unusually sustained for an early Beatle number, with long tied semibreves flowing into minims and into crotchet triplets. Here is a seed for later developments in Beatle music.

Perhaps we can sum up the appeal of these early songs in some such way as this:

Over and above the sheer physical impact they inherited from commercialised rock, they evoke a young happiness that haunts one because it is true; and is true because it's experience reborn into innocence. The technical manifestations of this are the songs' preoccupation with 'pure' folk-like melody (basically pentatonic and monodic) as against ordered harmony, with its Western, 'cultivated', associations: so that the vocal lines are marvellously fresh, whether with Paul's lyricism or John's toughness. The Beatles' music is more open, whiter, fresher, tenderer than the age-old black blues, for its Anglo-Irish affiliations lead it towards innocence rather than ecstasy, pleasure rather than pain, wholeness rather than blueness. Even the harmony provoked intuitively by modal melody and blue guitar techniques effects a kind of re-Renaissance – in wide-eyed, open-eared wonder at the 'pure' sensuality of thirds and sixths – strictly comparable with similar effects of harmonic 'discovery' in African musics (especially children's songs) and in the musics of Europe's late Middle Ages and early Renaissance. None the less, the ambivalence of the Negro blues, technically epitomised in the device of false relation – a clash between (harmonic) major third and (melodic-modal) minor third which is also a clash between cultures – is not entirely alien to Beatle music, even in their early days. Blue rawness and 'reality' temper their innocence; whilst their innocence transmutes aggression. It's this synthesis of qualities – American black and Anglo-Irish white – that makes the physical beat, which is their music's most *immediately* recognisable quality, a stimulus rather than a narcotic; and this again is what makes the happiness not mindlessly euphoric, but for real. The irony, or comedy, that often springs from this fusion is also pertinent here; the objectivity their songs achieve reconciles individual with corporate identity, and this helps to explain their tremendous impact on a whole generation. They were simply and sensuously affirmative; babes newborn, rejecting the past, yet singing for *dear life*.

None the less, because Beatle happiness was true, it had latent within it the awareness of pain and the negative emotions. This becomes evident in the deepening range of the songs that conclude their first period. Interestingly enough, these are associated with their first film, entitled *A Hard Day's Night*. To a consideration of this interfusion of light and dark we must proceed in the next chapter.

We have attempted to describe the Beatles' initiation, which is a ceremony of birth. On the next disc, *A hard day's night*, they're concerned with adolescence and growing up; and the rituals are those of puberty. The title song is another number about Love, identified with Home; but a more 'experienced' quality is evident in the verses, which use less youthfully abstract jargon, more down to earth fact. John has been 'working like a dog' to get money to buy his girl *things*. He should now, after his hard day, be 'sleeping like a log', but knows he won't be, because the things she'll do when he gets home will make him 'feel alright'. So there's again a division between innocence (the ecstasy of being 'held tight') and experience (things, making money, the tedium of work, suggested by the long repeated notes in the tune's first phrase). Both poetically and musically, however, this is subtler, because more equivocal, than in any previous song. Indeed one might say that the song sees innocence and experience as interdependent; the freedom couldn't be so lovely were it not for the tedium. This is incarnate in the music: which begins apparently in C major, though the opening sustained chord is arrestingly a dominant ninth of F, and the C major triads at the beginning of the tune sound more like dominants in F than tonics in C. The syncopated upward lift at the end of the phrase (on the word 'working') lurches us on to the flattened seventh; and the first strain consists, indeed, mainly of oscillations between a (merely latent) tonic of C and the flat seventh triad of B flat. The answering phrase, about getting home to her, balances this modality with descending chromatics in the tune, dominant sevenths and a very blue cadential false relation in the harmony. He actually reaches home in the 'middle' section on the *sharpened* seventh, but with a modal alternation of III I triads. The coda is deeply touching. He 'feels alright', he says, vacillating between a C major triad and its blue minor third, with subdominant

harmony also involving flattened sevenths: which then unexpectedly swing to a protracted, decorated triad of B flat, which
finally floats back (acting as flat seventh) to a C major triad. In
the recorded performance there is in fact *no* end, only a fade-out.

Ex. 7

There's nothing comparable with this effect in the textbook
harmony of the eighteenth or nineteenth century: though such
modally derived progressions are common in the music of the
sixteenth century and earlier – especially in keyboard music, since
cadential perorations like this lie easily 'under the fingers'. Of
course such processes in Beatle music are entirely empirical, as
to a large extent they were in the music of the Renaissance.
What matters is the intuitive subtlety of their effect; in this song
the coda crystallises the ambivalence between Home and World
Outside, for that floating B flat triad is a dream of bliss, if you
like, but it's a dream won through to by the blue reality of those
false relations. It's a small but meaningful detail that the repeated
G's in the vocal phrase, on the words 'I feel alright', anticipate
the lovely-surprising harmonic cadence: for whereas the first two

'alrights' oscillate between major and minor thirds, the last 'alright' stays still on the note G – which acts both as the fifth of the tonic C and as an added sixth to the triad of B flat. The repeated G's, which in the initial phrase spelt tedium ('work all day'), now suggest peace.

John and Paul share the vocal in *A hard day's night:* as they do in John's *If I fell*. Significantly, this is a song not only about love, but also about responsibility; and the equivocation between melody and harmony we observed in *A hard day's night* here takes a more explicit form. The pop standard convention of preludial 'verse' plus chorus in ABA form (usually in eight bar periods) is surprisingly re-created: for the verse begins chromatically off-key, and the side-stepping dominant sevenths hint at the 'wonder' of falling in love, realising that it entails more than holding hands, or even coition. The chorus, having *discovered* its tonic B flat, becomes rhythmically rigid, almost tranced, as he sings of giving his heart, the bass moving serenely parallel with the tune, with an unexpected mediant triad on the word 'heart' that is wonderingly tender rather than assertive. (Harmony text books used to designate the mediant as 'weak' and better avoided!) The strict repetition of the opening phrase

Ex. 8

emphasises the sense of dedication, almost of ceremonial. But the middle section, which has six bars instead of eight or four, and is initiated by a surprising chord of the ninth, makes us aware that there's duality and potential pain in this love experience, for there seems to be Another Woman who has hurt him, and who'll be hurt. The pain will be just bearable if the new love is for real and for ever; but the pain none the less exists, provoking dark subdominant minor triads, and a slightly more agitated rhythm. The equilibrium between this pain and the trance-like symmetry and euphony of the initial phrase is delicately sustained, and epitomised in the final, flattened, plagal cadence, which says Amen.

I'm happy to dance with you (John's number, but written for and sung by George) offers an interesting variation on the old Eden theme. The tune of the first strain is pure pentatonic in C: though the rumba-like nervosity of the rhythm (African cum Latin American) perhaps belies the simple happiness, as do the chromatic passing chords when he holds her hand. He then admits there may be Another Man, or men; but says 'let's just pretend that we can't see his face'. The words, however, are wide awake in thus sweeping nastiness under the carpet; and the music follows suit, partly through its rhythmic jitteriness, partly through its teetering between melodic-modal C minor and diatonic E flat major, with a IV V I cadence, juicily chromaticised at that. The coda's ululating 'Ohs' in rumba rhythm are thus ambiguous in effect, happy 'ohs' and unhappy 'ows', simultaneously.

This is an almost-comic song with painful ironic undertones. John's *Any time at all* is apparently a straight love song saying that he'll never fail her, in any sense. Yet it's no dreamy wish-fulfilment number, but – as powerfully sung by John – tough, hard, resilient. It opens with a primitive pentatonic 'tumbling strain' such as is familiar in American Indian as well as Negro music;

Ex. 9

it is sustained by a driving dotted rhythm; and is riddled with painfully blue sevenths. The tonality wavers between B flat major and an aeolian G minor; the chromatic flattening in the bass, when he asks her to look into his eyes, emphasises the song's rock-bottom *reality*. This is one of the blackest, most Negroid of early Beatle songs, directly recalling not only the blues but, more decisively, the Gospel shout.

The starkness of this song provides a transition to Paul's *Things we said today*, for me the Beatles' most beautiful and deep song up to this point. Again it concerns the reality of love, involving responsibility and wonder as well as pleasure. A fierce drumbeat introduces the opening strain which is unambiguously pentatonic, undulating around a nodal G with never a hint of a sharp seventh. The rhythm is grave, the percussion almost minatory, the vocal tessitura restricted, while the harmony oscillates between triads of G minor and D minor. The flavour is incantatory, even liturgical, a moment outside Time. The second strain hints at the possibility of loss, with a weeping chromatic descent in triplet rhythm, and with rapid but dreamy tonal movement flowing from B flat by way of a rich dominant ninth to E flat: the subdominant triad of which then serves as a kind of Neapolitan cadence drooping back (without the linking dominant) to the grave pentatonic G minor (see Ex. 10). In the middle section the gravity acquires a somewhat tremulous passion. The pulse beats quicker, quietly thudding in regular quavers: whilst the vocal line is consistently offbeat, with false relations and sequential sevenths. The chromatics and the rhythmic instability don't allow the major key to be decisively established: so although this middle section *hints* at the turbulence of passion it doesn't radically disturb – though it certainly deepens – the effect of the da capo of the pentatonic incantation. Indeed this song makes incarnate the Beatles' truth to experience. The words tell us little by themselves, for the point is precisely that the love-experience is too deep for words: 'Someday when we're dreaming, deep in love, not a lot to say, Then we will remember Things we said today.' The music, with its faintly liturgical flavour, genuinely acts this out, creating an experience

Ex. 10

no longer just happy, but full of awe. Here the fade-out legitimately carries us outside Time.

There's a comparable development in John's *When I get home*, if one compares it with earlier homing songs. The key is an aeolian E minor oscillating to a diatonic G major; but the excitement inherent in the getting home to her finds outlet not merely in the driving beat but still more in the sudden eruptions of E major triads in 'African' antiphony. These E major yells (on an abracadabra 'song of the vowels') are at once liberating and surprising: so that the music comes out as joyful, but fear-full. This is a tougher, 'maturer' permutation of the fusion of innocence with vulnerability we noticed in earlier songs.

John also wrote and sings *I'll be back*, which is about the possibility of betrayal and is, significantly, one of the bluest of early Beatle songs, in feeling if not form. It's triggered off by a tension between a rising pentatonic G major phrase on guitar for the loving and a leaping *minor* sixth for the breaking heart.

Although the rising sixth becomes major when, in the 'middle' section (which John says is 'a bit tarty') he threatens to run away, a gravely fierce G minor is reasserted in the da capo and coda, which ends loud, but bluely unresolved. *I'll cry instead* is another song of loss and betrayal, in which the lyrical Paul joins John. But it complements *I'll be back* in being comically deflatory. Like the banjo-strumming, eupeptic Country-Western music which it emulates, it will have no truck with pain. Unlike the music of a Frank Proffitt, however, it's ironically aware of its heartless and mindless insouciance, so its gaiety is less crass, more enlivening. John's exuberant singing of *You can't do that* completes the process of liberating the 'negative' emotions. Almost for the first time it's an anti-love song which generates a kind of joy from the recognition of betrayal. The melismata are tipsily ecstatic, the textures very blue. This must be one of the first songs obsessively to exploit the *simultaneous* sounding of major and minor thirds. The repeated quavers nag, if somewhat comically: and the

Ex. 11

middle section's sudden shift (on the word 'green') to the sharp seventh of the relative is an explosion. So the song is at once a threat and an assertion of identity, the me against the rest and against the togetherness of love. This embryonically anticipates the Beatles' second period.

The next disc, *Beatles for Sale*, contains songs that develop the themes we've just touched on. Thus John's *No reply* is again about betrayal, only it's wistful, and at once tough and comic

rather than – like *You can't do that* – perversely ecstatic. The
verses describe a situation, eschewing all ornament:

> *This happened once before when I came to your door*
> *No reply*
> *They said it wasn't you but I saw you peep through*
> *Your window.*
> *I saw the light*
> *I know that you saw me cos I looked up to see*
> *Your face.*

There are virtually no descriptive words; yet the suburban house
is as vividly evoked as the little drama within, in which the word
'peep' functions half comically, half fearfully. This gets into the
music too, for the symmetrical rhythm and simple, scalewise
rise and fall of the tune's opening phrase are deflated by the
pentatonic roulade – preceded by a silence – for 'no reply'.
'Innocent' African thirds, yelled antiphonally, help him to 'see
the light', which is punningly generated both by the wall-switch
and by his recognition of the truth. The middle section preserves
the rhythmic symmetry but gets swept tonally off-centre by her
lies (on a very sharp mediant triad of B major, leading to E, major
of the relative of the home key G). Another wistful-comic approach
to the theme of loss occurs in *Baby's in black*, an odd little song
halfway between a child's rune and a music-hall ditty, altogether
remote from the blues. Baby's in black because she's grieving
for a lost lover who won't come back, so Paul's lovesick lyricism
forlornly bleats 'Oh dear what can I do' in triplets that distantly
recall 'O dear what can the matter be'. But the song's naïve
dismay is modified by the sequential sevenths in the harmony
(the flat seventh approach to the subdominant triad is ineffably
doleful) and by a rhythmic irregularity whereby the first four-bar
phrase is balanced by a truncated three-bar phrase. The middle
has two bars only, with no 'contrasting' phrase, though there is a
momentary modulation to the dominant. After the da capo we're
left suspended, as the 'What can I do' echoes into silence.

A positive development towards tenderness and compassion is
evident in Paul's beautiful *I'll follow the sun*. Again, this is about

loss; but he's leaving her of his own volition, and since he's following the *sun* away from the rain, the loss is presumably also gain – a move upwards. So the song isn't flagrantly assertive in its independence, like *You can't do that*; neither is it plaintively childish, like *Baby's in black*. It manages to be at once hopeful (the unusual shape of the seven-bar opening period is built on syncopated rising fourths, perfect, imperfect, perfect, with the implied flatwards modulation from B flat to A flat immediately cancelled by a sharpwards modulation to the dominant):

Ex. 12

and at the same time resigned (the flat subdominants in the second section, the declining melisma on 'oh'). Each time we return to a new stanza the abrupt shift from E flat (with minor colouring) back to B flat major is a surprise. The song is wide awake – those rising fourths really do reach for the sun – yet paradoxically chaste, lyrical but cool.

What you're doing – said by John to be one of the rare joint compositions – also discovers a somewhat distraught lyricism in an apparently 'negative' situation. The first strain consists simply of triads of tonic alternating with subdominant plus flattened seventh – which makes a blue false relation with the tonic triad. The vocal line, enclosed within a fifth, stabs in misplaced accents. The middle section, telling how he's been waiting for her unavailingly, is more lyrically sustained, but the upward thrusting pentatonic phrase breaks off, breathless. Though it modulates with increased energy to the dominant, it immediately subsides in a drooping melisma. The beat is quick, brittle, impatient; and the interlude for electric organ acquires an almost sinister resonance.

If this is also an erotic song (though impure rather than pure), John's *I don't want to spoil the party* is relatively homely. He's going to leave the party because She isn't there. Though he's sad because he still loves her – and the long semibreves to which these words are sung suggest that he means them – he's clearly not, as was Paul in *What you're doing*, deeply disturbed. Interestingly enough, the greater sophistication of the song – in diatonic music-hall, George Formbyish vein – makes it emotionally less involved. It's funny and clever, and the modulation to the relative minor gives point to that 'what went wrong'; but only when he leaves, and a flattened seventh unexpectedly intrudes into the cadence, is there a hint of real involvement. Of course, the brisk façade is itself a kind of truth, for the song is precisely concerned with Keeping Up Appearances.

Help, incorporating songs from the Beatles' second film, includes fine numbers in one or another of the old manners, and the title song (by John), is one of them. The first words are 'When I was younger'; and it's about how, in growing up,

Ex. 13

one comes to rely more, not less, on other people, especially on lovers. The familiar mediant transitions and flat sevenths are potently employed; and the coda's frenzied-comic yell for help is an alternation of tonic triads with submediants. *You're going to lose that girl*, ebulliently sung by John, makes disturbing contrast between the pentatonic first strain (with an incipient modulation to the relative minor that fails to materialise) and wild modulations in the middle section wherein he threatens to take the girl away from his pal: a lurch from F minor 7 to D flat, with a suggestion of B flat minor, then to C flat and G flat triads which shift abruptly to E major (see Ex. 13). Though the modulations are initiated by melodic movement, empirically, there's nothing to match their violence in the earlier songs. *You've got to hide your love away* is a new departure in a directly contrary sense. It has no connection with jazz and little with the blues. A slowly swaying incantation in 12/8, the tune moves up from the tonic through a fourth, then down again, entirely without modulation and with purely triadic harmony. The modal false relations are more like Vaughan Williams (or his sixteenth-century forebears) that the blues. John hides his love away, becoming a holy fool or clown, because the world destroys truth. This anticipates the fool-songs of the third period (see Ex. 14).

There's a somewhat similar effect in Paul's *Tell me what you see*, which is specifically about communication – if you can really open your eyes, what you'll see is me. But what is remarkable is the simplicity with which communication is effected. The four-bar periods are symmetrical, the harmony is restricted to diatonic concords of tonic and subdominant with one cadential dominant; yet the leaping octave at the beginning, and the syncopation on 'break your heart', open the ears, catch the breath, creating a little revelation. Perhaps such inspired simplicity was necessary before the small miracle of *Yesterday* could be achieved. Paul has lost his girl, and although the opening *words* tell us that yesterday his troubles seemed far away, the *music* in the second bar immediately enacts these troubles with a disquieting modulation from tonic, by way of the sharpened sixth, to the relative. The first bar, with its gentle sigh, seems separated,

Ex. 14

1. Here   I   stand   with head   in   hand__
2. Ev - 'ry-where   peo - ple stare__
3. How   can   I   ev - en   try__
4. How   could she   say   to me__

turn   my face   to the wall
each   and   ev-'ry day
I   can   nev-er win
love   will   find a way

stranded, by the abrupt modulation; and although the troubles
'return to stay' with a descent to the tonic, the anticipated modulation sharpwards is counteracted when the B natural is flattened to
make an irresolute plagal cadence (see Ex. 15). The 'lost' feeling
is incarnate in the irregular phrasing: for that one isolated bar is
followed by two, and then by two plus two. This makes seven,
leaving us one bar short; but this first irregular strain is completed
by the tune's continuation after the double bar: which also, of
course, initiates the middle section. In itself this consists of a four-
bar phrase in the relative minor, wonderingly repeated to fill out
the words, which forlornly 'don't know why she wouldn't stay'
(because she 'wouldn't say'). But the 'lost' bar remains lost, so
stability is never established; and the hesitant irregularity of the

Ex. 15

Moderato (Gently)

Yes - ter - day
Sud - den - ly

all my trou - bles seemed so far a - way
I'm not half the man I used to be

Now it looks as though they're here to stay Oh
There's a sha - dow hang - ing ov - er me Oh

I be - lieve___ in yes - ter - day___
yes - ter - day___ came sud - den - ly___

first clause seems the more poignant on its return. The immediate nostalgia of the song is without suspicion of sentimentality, and the corny accompaniment of string quartet can be employed, with validity, to reinforce the music's frail bewilderment. The use of the violin obbligato is, indeed, subtle. Though it sings, as strings must, it doesn't indulgently soar; and at the moment when one expects it to take off it stays quite still, on a long inverted pedal, thereby inducing a wide-eyed wonder, with a tinge of apprehension (when will it move, or cease?). If George Martin (the Beatles' producer) is responsible for this, it none the less betrays so infallible an insight into the imaginative heart of Beatle music that one assumes some telepathic empathy between Martin and the composing Beatles. Certainly what happens in the instrumental parts in this song is inconceivably remote from what would have been done by the average commercial arranger.

In any case, the naïve-sentimental scoring underlines the 'lost' quality on which we've commented in melody, harmony and structure. Being lost, the song tells us, is part of the painful process of growing up. He believes in yesterday, as we all do, because then love was 'an easy game to play'. Now he needs a 'place to hide away' from the shadow; and with the words 'O yesterday came suddenly', the sense is inverted, for 'yesterday' becomes the recognition of the shadow itself, the moment of truth. Negatively, one can attribute this merely to the slack syntax which the Beatles share with all pop lyricists, the words trickling or spurting out to fit, or help to make, the tune. Positively, one can regard it as a beautiful example of the functioning of an 'oral' poetry which is pre-syntactical, and in which the emotional ambivalence is the kind of accident that may happen to an intuitive artist. As the Beatles grow up, such accidents occur with increasing frequency; and there is probably no precedent for this outside relatively primitive folk cultures. Baby Mozart, or even teenage Schubert, didn't function thus empirically, since they worked within a stable and literate tradition. Mozart seems miraculously to have missed out on puberty; Schubert's teenage songs do not noticeably differ, in the range of their themes or even their technical sophistication, from those of his maturity.

The next disc, *Rubber Soul*, is not a new departure, though its punning title hints at greater flexibilities of irony and compassion. The lyrics – especially John's – are wittier than ever before; but their ability to make us laugh, sometimes out loud, doesn't discredit tenderness. The first song, *Drive my car*, is a fine example of this: an anti-girl song in which the humour is unhurtful. 'Asked a girl what she wanted to be, She said "Baby can't you see? I wanna be famous, a star of the screen, But you can do something in between. Baby, you can drive my car, and maybe I'll love

Ex. 16

you".' She's gently guyed in the first strain, talking in speech rhythm, all on one note, over tonic and dominant drone with softly flattened sevenths. This static phrase contrasts with the 'Baby you can drive my car' refrain, which is a dominant arpeggio over a mediant triad, syncopating its D natural to a D flat, and driving the car out in a triplet melisma. The energy of this surprises, after the first strain's amused detachment; but then the phrase is rounded off, on 'and maybe I'll love you', with a return to pentatonic lyricism (see Ex. 16). The coda, however, with a 'music of the vowels' for the beep-beeping motor car, is unadulterated comedy or even farce. All these ironies touchingly create a whole, for if the girl's ambitions are satirically presented in the one-note verse, the 'drive my car' refrain delicately hints at love's potential; whilst the 'maybe I'll love you' throw-away conclusion, wavering between flat and sharp seventh, is just right, leaving us in no doubt that love is good, yet refusing (whether tactfully or nervously) final commitment. And of course, the ironies are an admission of reality: the star-struck girl proves to have *no* car, though it looks as though she may have a driver, 'and that's a start'.

John's *Norwegian wood* is another anti-girl song that tells a story, though John has hinted, some years later, that like most of his best songs it's autobiographical. This time there's a hint of class consciousness in the irony, which may be why the song is less generous. The girl in her elegant Norwegian-wooded apartment is strong on social, weak on sexual, intercourse; her polished archness is satirised in an arching waltz tune wearily fey, yet mildly surprising because in the mixolydian mode (see Ex. 17). Here the flat seventh gives to the comedy an undercurrent of wistfulness, and this embraces both John's frustration and the girl's pretentiousness – which is pointed by George's playing the sitar, not in emulation of Indian styles, but as an exotic guitar. The middle section brings us to the crux of the situation (which is, for John, a night spent in the bath) with a stern intrusion of the tonic minor triad and a tune descending, with drooping appoggiatura, to the subdominant with flattened seventh. After this middle the lyricism of the waltz da capo suggests not so much

Ex. 17

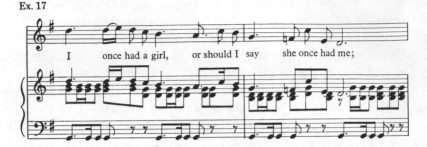

plaintiveness as a comic dismay. The effect of the flattened
seventh, followed by a rise through a fifth and a fall through a
sixth, pendulum-like, even seems a trifle sinister in context: as
perhaps it is, if 'I lit a fire, isn't it good, Norwegian wood' implies
a slight case of arson.

John's *Nowhere Man* also tells us that it isn't manners that
maketh man (or woman). Sung by John and Paul, it's a less
specifically ironic portrait, first presenting the man who is 'as
blind as he can be, just sees what he wants to see' in barber-shop
close harmony, unaccompanied, then in four bars of hymnbook
diatonicism I V IV I. The middle, asking Nowhere Man if he
knows what he's missing, is both more modal and more lyrical,
with insidious mediant triads. This deepens the satire on the
socialite or all-too-civil servant who's afraid of emotional commitment; and at the same time underlines the twist in the refrain
which – approaching the cadence by way of the flattened subdominant – asks whether Nowhere Man isn't 'a bit like you and
me'. It would seem that the prevalence of 'anti' songs on this

disc may be an inverted positive – a move towards self-reliance, in reaction to the Nowhere Man. Certainly John's *Run for your life*, a totally explicit anti-girl song, generates a joyous exuberance from its mediant alternations, so that its brusqueness is not synonymous with cruelty. Similarly, Paul's *I'm looking through you* pierces through pretences as it answers its upward flowing phrases with a resigned descent from the subdominant's flat seventh: whilst George's *If I needed someone* effects an act of rejection by way of an obsessive tugging to the *chord* of the flat seventh. In all these songs there's a toughness, beneath lyricism or comedy, that is not evident in earlier songs.

The best songs on *Rubber Soul* are not, however, overtly satirical; certainly the anti-girl elements in John's *Girl* are complemented by a lyricism so touching in its simplicity that the ironies take us by surprise. Again we see how the remarkable development in Beatle verse, wherein 'reality' and wit are interdependent, is inseparable from the comparable development in their music, which in this song is simultaneously funny and pathetic. The opening strain presents the girl with almost balladic impersonality ('Is there anybody goin' to listen to my story All about the girl who came to stay'). Yet the tune – in an aeolian-sounding C minor, with regular, gently arching quavers followed by rocking fourths and thirds – is heart-easingly lovely, and isn't destroyed by the almost-comic pentatonic refrain 'Ah girl', which sighfully and unexpectedly droops to E flat major (see Ex. 18). The middle, however, veers abruptly to the minor of the supertonic of E flat (or the subdominant of C minor), and the fetching tune is abandoned in favour of regularly repeated quavers on the syllable tit-tit (which sometimes sounds like tut-tut!). As the lyricism is banished, so the girl is deflated: from being a girl in a storybook she's become a flesh-and-blood, immensely desirable young woman; who now turns out to be 'the kind of girl who puts you down when friends are there'. The melismata are 'cool', the sighs verge on the ludicrous; yet this paradoxically intensifies the loving pathos of the lyrical tune when it's sung da capo, since life is a tangled mesh of hopes and disappointments. Though the verses are in themselves charming, they can reveal their depth only

Ex. 18

Moderately slow

1. Is there an-y-bo-dy going to lis-ten to my sto - ry,

All a-bout the girl who came to stay, She's the

kind of girl you want so much it makes you sor - ry,

Still you don't re-gret a sin-gle day. Ah GIRL

in association with the music. This is a beautiful example of how the durability of Beatle songs depends on their unassuming truth. The hurt inherent in living, as well as loving, is accepted without pretention, yet without rancour.

So it's not surprising that the Beatles can still, on occasion, sing straight celebrative love songs. In Paul's *Michelle* (though John helped with the middle), the model is French cabaret song rather than Negro blues or Anglo-Irish folk or music-hall. Yet this is also a runic song in that the point is that the girl, being French, can't intellectually comprehend English, so he must sing to her in a 'music of the vowels', which is also the language of love. Harmonically, this is very sophisticated for a Beatle song, with tender chromatic sequences and tritonal intrusions in the melody when he says 'These are words that go together'. None the less, the words that really matter are those that are talismantic; and the 'I love you' refrain, in swaying triplets, is pure pentatonic love-call. The subtlety of the song lies in the contrast between chromatic sophistication (both in the tune and, in the middle section, in the bass) and pentatonic innocence; and this duality is already hinted at in the first two bars' false relations between F major and D flat triads. The F major sounds as though it's

Ex. 19

going to be a dominant to B flat minor. This never materialises, though there's always a plagal, flattened feeling about the cadences into F major. This gives a tentative, exploratory quality to the tenderness, hinting that the barrier isn't just one of language, but is inherent in the separateness of each individual, however loving. It is this, I suspect, which safeguards the song from over-sweetness.

Two other love songs are utterly remote from sweetness. *Wait*, another song about coming home, has no overt irony, though it does suggest 'a recognition of other modes of experience that are possible'. The upwards lilting arpeggio, followed by rumba-syncopation on tonic minor and dominant ninths, conveys expectancy, excitement, but also hesitation, apprehension and doubt, which the B flat major trumpet arpeggio in the second strain ebulliently releases. The return to the first phrase is by way of a passing chord of the thirteenth on 'tears', so the song is held in tense equilibrium, potently truthful. The middle is not

Ex. 20

built on contrasting material, though it introduces tonal movement by way of sequential sevenths. *The word*, a joint composition, sung by John and Paul, with George in the refrain, is a ritual love-spell, with rudimentary tonic and subdominant triads accompanying a love-call rising upwards in parallel thirds, then descending. The tonic minor triads formed by the voice part are underpinned by false related tonic major triads in the guitars, giving the song a runic wildness; and false relations between triads of D major and B flat major occur too, syncopated, in the descending answering phrase:

Ex. 21

This gives the simple words – 'It's so fine, it's sunshine' – an unexpected resonance; and prepares us for the four-bar middle, which sets the words 'in the beginning' to a priestly monotone, undulating between triads a tone apart – 'non-temporal' flat sevenths, neither achieving nor seeking cadential resolution. So the Word that is evoked may be Love, with overtly sexual implications in the upward thrusting arpeggio and the lacerating false relations; yet the sacramental connotations of the Word are also latent, since the song's potency is grave, almost austere, in its modality.

This little song is of some importance in the Beatles' development, for the magical and runic qualities which we have seen to be implicit in many of their early songs here become explicit. In their Hard Day's Night they've learned that love isn't the simple boy-meets-girl relationship it had seemed to be; at least the feelings released by such basic heterosexual contacts are both confused and confusing: inseparable from other people and the 'world outside': inseparable, it would seem, from metaphysical as well as physical sanctions, using the term literally and without pretention. Inevitably, there's a tie-up between the widening range of the Beatles' experience and the expansion of their technical resources. In any case, their next disc, *Revolver*, is at once a break-through in technique and a new kind of experience.

Part Two
Contest
and Death

3. Revolvers in Penny Lane and Strawberry Fields

Though *Revolver* still contains ritual elements, one can no longer discuss it in terms of adolescent ceremonial, nor is it relatable to the conventions of commercialised pop music. Halfway between ritual and art, it's both verbally and musically an extraordinary break-through; and since the songs complement one another without exactly forming a sequence, one cannot avoid some comment on each.

Rather surprisingly, George Harrison starts off with an overtly satirical song, *Taxman*. This has nothing to do with Love and is in a way a protest song, since it assumes that there is and must be an inevitable and eternal battle between Taxman-Establishment and Me: which cannot end except with death ('Declare the pennies on your eyes'). So George sets it as a fiercely driving barrelhouse boogie, with a consistently pentatonic tune and an ostinato bass that is constant throughout (see Ex. 22). Though there are two sharps in the D major key signature, the sharpened leading note is in fact never needed. Most of the song rides over a tonic pedal, the only other chords being the plagal subdominant, the triad on the flattened seventh, and one flattened mediant in the coda. George sings it with a powerfully felt jazz impetus, whereby *all* the stresses are slightly displaced – an effect cunningly combining weariness with exasperation. There are some aggressively blue false relations, especially when the other Beatles respond to George antiphonally. Earlier Beatle songs had attained greater dionysiac fervour, but not this hard-edged toughness which manages to be melancholy and resiliently comic at the same time. This duality the song shares with genuine barrelhouse music; and the primitivism is intensified by the raucous, savagely amplified organ, pentatonically doodling like an old-style boogie player such as Romeo Nelson, at once hot and coolly detached. Having no 'leading note' the song doesn't end but fades away;

Ex. 22

it *leads* nowhere, because Mr. Taxman (yesterday called Mr.
Wilson, today Mr. Heath) is there always.

The second song, *Eleanor Rigby*, is mostly by Paul and complements the first by being its polar opposite. *Taxman* is an
anti-love song; *Eleanor Rigby* is pro-love, though it's not a love
song in the sense that the majority of early Beatle songs were.
It's about compassion, loneliness, and implicitly about the
generation gap – three basic themes of second period Beatle
music – and there is no precedent for its musical idiom, which has
nothing to do with jazz, but is an amalgam of rural folk and urban
music-hall. The tonality is a dorian E minor, though the initial
invocation of 'all the lonely people' is a rising and falling scale
(with sharpened fourth) over a C major triad, with a rocking and
chugging accompaniment. The song proper is narrative ballad,
and the words are poetry, evoking with precise economy Eleanor
Rigby, the middle-aged spinster who picks up the rice at somebody

else's wedding, lives in a dream, keeps her face 'in a jar by the door'; and Father Mackenzie, the priest who lives alone, darns his socks in the empty night, writes the sermon that no one wants to listen to, wipes off his hands the dirt from the grave where he's buried Eleanor Rigby after administering the last rites by which 'no one was saved'. The words reverberate through their very plainness; and manage to characterise not merely these two lonely people but also (as George Melly has put it) the 'big soot-black sandstone Catholic churches with the trams rattling past, the redbrick terraced houses with laced curtains and holy-stoned steps' of the Beatles' boyhood Liverpool. The tune, lyrically sung by Paul, never modulates but has a tentative, groping tenderness as it stretches up the scale to those modally sharpened sixths, only to droop again, in a flexible rhythm that often overrides the barlines: so when it returns to the choric introductory phrase as a refrain, the scope of the song is marvellously extended. Miss Rigby and Father Mackenzie, the soaring refrain tells us, may be founded on real characters from the Beatles' childhood, yet none the less represent *all* the lonely people: and that includes us, and the young Beatles (who were soon to be members of Sgt. Pepper's LONELY HEARTS club band). Yet there is never a suspicion of emotional indulgence in the song; that is belied by the rigidity of the chugging accompaniment, even though it is given to emotive strings. Occasionally (after that dismayed octave leap for 'where *do* they all come from') the violins wing up scalewise; more often they reinforce the thumping crotchet pulse, or the rocking quavers. In the final phrase of the tune and in the coda the 'where do they all come from' query reaches up not through an octave but a tenth (see Ex. 23). This makes something like a climax, and the song has an end which is not, however, decisive. The final cadence is the only V I progression in the piece, and even here the dominant chord is in second inversion. All the other cadences reinforce the tonal ambiguity of the submediant introduction, an effect the more disturbing because the C major triads conflict with the sharpened Cs in the modal tune.

These first two songs, one in a negative, the other in a positive sense, are about Them and Us. With the next song John Lennon

Ex. 23

is concerned with the Me: for *I'm only sleeping* is the first of the
sequence of dream songs that equate reality with the 'world
within'. Also in a modal E minor (aeolian this time), it begins
with reiterated Es in boogie rhythm, knocking on the doors of
consciousness as he lies, between sleeping and waking, in the
early morning light. The tune itself, however, as he 'floats
upstream', is beautifully expansive, unfolding in a rising sixth,
then drooping in rather uneasy, syncopated stresses until it
comes to rest swinging between tonic and fifth (see Ex. 24).
Here triads of E minor and C major are telescoped and left unresolved: until there's a sudden, very loud E minor triad, succeeded
by silence. This momentarily wakes him up, for in the middle
section (which moves in boogie rhythm from E minor to an
ambiguous tonality that turns out to be A minor) he's lying half
awake, 'keeping an eye on the world' (in descending chromatics),
though again wooing sleep and dream. The blissfully lilting,
rising sixth tune returns da capo, but so does the ambiguous
cadence and the thumping E minor triad. So the song remains

Ex. 24

Leave me where I am I'm on - ly

sleep - ing.

delicately balanced between the reality within and the reality outside the mind: in somewhat the same way as *Eleanor Rigby* manages to be at once compassionate and dispassionate.

It's interesting that this incipient dream-song immediately preceded the Beatles' first unambiguous exploration of orientalism. For George Harrison's *Love you too* a real Indian sitar and tabla player are called in, allowed to improvise preludially, and then incorporated into a Beatle incantation or love-spell. In this song there is, of course, no harmony, in the Western sense, only a tonic and dominant drone over which sitar and voice embroider melismatically. The vocal line oscillates around G, moving up to B flat, the flattened seventh, down to F natural; and the music convinces not because it is 'like' genuine Indian music (it is by Indian standards rudimentary), but because it is an extension of the anti-Western, anti-materialism, anti-action theme we have seen to be endemic in Beatle music. Though George seems to be singing (as did all the early Beatle songs) of sexual love and presumably of coitus itself, his point is that the act of love can destroy the temporal sense ('make love all day, make love singing songs'): which is what happens in the drone-coda and fade-out.

Paul's *Here there and everywhere* returns to more familiar Beatle territory, for it's a straight heterosexual love lyric with an apparently simple G major tune, sung by Paul in his most ingratiating vein. The simplicity is, however, deceptive, since the song is about love as revelation, and the tune has affinities with the lyrical passages of John's dream song, *I'm only sleeping*. The lovely initial phrase, rising through a ninth, descending to the fifth, enacts the 'change' in his life created by a mere wave of the girl's hand. And the metamorphosis happens tonally and

Ex. 25

metrically also, first in the syncopated modulations to F sharp minor 7 and B 7, then in the shifting mediant modulations and asymmetrical five and a half bar phrase of the middle section, which overlaps the da capo. The final plagal cadence is an Amen.

If *Love you too* tells us how the love-experience erases time,

Here there and everywhere obliterates place. Typically, the Beatles
then torpedo this lyrical tenderness with a *Yellow submarine*, of
which Paul wrote the chorus and John 'helped with the blunder-
buss bit'. After Paul's light tenor, Ringo's blunt Liverpudlianism
brings us back to earth, or anyway to 'the town where I was
born', in a rhythm as strictly circumscribed, a diatonicism as
plain, as that of the Celebrated Working Men's Band. Yet the
banality is as deceptive as was the simplicity of *Here, there and
everywhere*. For the song turns out to be a revocation of childhood
memory that is also a liberation into dream – an 'instant nursery
rhyme', as George Melly has put it, 'as unselfconscious as a
children's street song, but true to their own experience . . . It's
not American comic book heroes who climb aboard the Yellow
Submarine but Desperate Dan and Lord Snooty and his pals.
The departure for the Sea of Dreams is from the Liverpool
pierhead.' One might even say that the song's *human* triviality
sets off the mystery of the 'aquatic unknown tongues' we then
hear bobbing on and in the waters: in which sense regression is
prelude to another rebirth. If there's nothing in the music that
is memorable in itself – except the fact that it's easy to memorise
and so stays in the mind – we're soon aware that the experience
isn't, and isn't meant to be, purely musical. A hubbub of friends
is heard on the quay, the town band blares its blatant farewell,
and we're in a mythical world – to be more deeply explored in
Sgt. Pepper – which cannot be adequately 'realised' in concert
hall or on stage. The music has, again, a talismantic function,
recalling a Liverpudlian childhood, launching the Beatles on a
submarine voyage into the unconscious: out of which their later
and greater music was to spring.

   There's hint of this, in a negative sense, in the very curious
song, *She said she said* that concludes side 1. John says it was
triggered off by Peter Fonda's remarking, on a drug trip, that he
knew what it was like to be dead; but it comes out as a conversation
between John and an (I suspect) older woman, who might be a
failed lover – or mother or aunt. She says she knows 'what it's
like to be dead', he says she's making him feel 'like he's never
been born'. Abrupt changes of metre from double to triple time

suggest mutual incomprehension; and in the triple rhythmed section he tells us that 'when I was a boy, everything was right'. Verbally, the song is a mysterious example of 'oral' poetry; musically, it is totally without development, rotating around itself. The harmony is restricted to triads of tonic, subdominant and flat seventh; and the A flat triads, thumping into the basic B flat, are always a disruption, both harmonically and rhythmically. The only passage that flows easily is the boyhood bit in the middle, which is *in* the sub-dominant. When the da capo occurs he says he knows that he's 'ready to leave' (because she makes him feel as though he's never been born). But the original rising fifth and scale figure don't acquire more impetus with these more hopeful words, still being yanked down by that heavy, flat seventh triad; and there's no end to the song, only a slow fade-out as the other Beatles echo 'I know what it's like to be dead, I know what it's like to be sad'.

After that, it's a joy to begin side 2 with a resurgence of McCartney lyricism. *Good day sunshine* is, however, an extraordinary song, answerable to no precedent. A hammering of F major triads seems to be a subdominant prelude to a C major refrain, chorically sung in ecstatic rumba rhythm; but that surprisingly leads, by way of subdominant triads with flattened sevenths, into B flat major: which proves to be the key of the tune, infectiously happy in boogie rhythm, with blue flat seventh on a high A flat. The tune is a brief yodel equating the love experience with the sunny day; the middle section is instrumental, in barrelhouse style. The coda, however, hoists us up from B flat to C, for a repeat of the invocation to the sun. Again the subdominants turn into dominant sevenths of B flat, but this time they're screwed up a further semitone to B major! (see Ex. 26). So the fade-out here generates a timeless, upward-lifting ecstasy. In *And your bird can sing* John deals with a similar theme, only with more equivocal irony – as one might expect. It's an appeal for communication, and in a sense for sacrifice, since if you are to get, see and hear me you must be prepared to get priorities right, dispensing with possessions and self-interest. The pounding beat and chattering thirds recall barrelhouse piano; and the 'sharp' E major tonality,

Ex. 26

with G sharp minor for the 'middle', seems to intensify the song's slightly scary flavour. It ends on a subdominant 6 4 unresolved: which would seem to make it the negative complement to Paul's Sunshine song, with more verbal but less musical interest.

Paul offers *his* negative song in *For no one*, but its melancholy is lyrically haunting. Though structurally a conventional 'standard', the song has something of the balladic feeling of *Eleanor Rigby*; and the opening eight-bar clause achieves a touching equilibrium between the cold breaking day and aching mind, and the memory of the lost love's 'words of kindness'. The bass descends evenly down the scale from tonic to subdominant, but then rises to the flat seventh to approach the cadence. This fall in the bass line, and the flattening of its harmonic implications, is counteracted by the melody which, at first motionless on a tentatively syncopated G, arches upwards triadically to E, and then descends, also triadically, through an octave (see Ex. 27). The harmonisation of the returned G with a B flat triad with added

Ex. 27

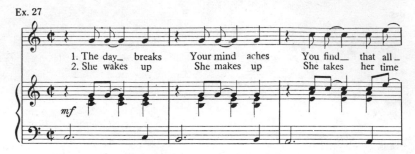

sixth conveys the desolation ('she no longer needs you') without
destroying the lyricism. The middle section sidesteps to the minor
of the supertonic – a melodic-modal procedure often found in
sixteenth-century dance pieces. A ballad-like, rocking accompaniment supports the tune which again describes a small arch – an
oddly fragmented four-bar phrase repeated, with an appendix of
two bars shifting gauchely back to the tonic. The C sharps of the
syncopated D minor cadence are contradicted by C naturals in the

declining phrase, which tell us that her tears cried 'for no-one'. In the da capo he can't believe that she no longer loves him: which gives depth to the tension between rising melody and falling bass. But the coda repeats the middle section complete, and then limply droops back from D minor to that dominant seventh of C, leaving us suspended. Again this sad little song – the tempo of which is unexpectedly brisk, given the nature of the words and lyricism of the melody – is remote from self-indulgence. The verse is touching oral poetry that extracts pathos from the very bareness of its statement – the eyes that 'see nothing, no sign of love behind the tears'; and this is precisely captured in the floating tune and irresolute harmonies, at once poignant and cool. Similarly Alan Civil's brilliant horn obbligato (which Paul is said to have burpled to George Martin) bubbles up ebulliently, yet manages to sound frailly sad, because precarious. It takes an Alan Civil to play it, of course, and this is another instance of the LP being an expansion both of technology and of artistic resource. The Beatles may call in whom they will; what matters is knowing what one wants – and having a George Martin on hand to produce the men and machines to make the ideal real.

Dr. Robert, a satirical song to complement *Taxman* is a Lennon song (but Paul helped in the middle), wry in tone but neither fierce nor peevish. The comedy is inherent in the ostinato rhythm, jazzy but with a suggestion of music-hall vamping: in the ambiguous tonality (A major with flattened sevenths): and in the side-stepping modulation to B minor. The middle section is lifted to B major, in arpeggiated minims, inanely smiling because we're 'feeling fine'. There's no end to the song, any more than to the ubiquitous taxman: though it's not clear whether Dr. Robert represents the medical profession in general, a bogus psychiatrist, or whether the satire isn't in part directed against his patients (including us).

George's number on side 2, *I want to tell you*, has no Eastern connotations, but is an oddly fragmented song, not surprisingly since it concerns the difficulty of communication. It opens with broken boogie rhythms and blue guitar phrases; and it's these instrumental forces that sunder recurrent attempts to create a

singing line. A savage attack of minor ninths over a dominant
pedal recalls the classical blues player, whilst sounding the fiercer
in plangent amplification. The phrasing is also wanderingly
irregular, a four-bar introduction being followed by a strain of
eleven bars (or ten plus an instrumental transition). The middle
section, which lifts us (without 'modulation') up a tone to B
minor-major, has seven bars, plus a bar of tonic fill-up to introduce
the da capo. The 'middle' oscillates around B and A, unable to
rise to a tune: but tells her that he doesn't 'mean to be unkind,
It's only me, it's not my mind'. In the da capo he says that he
feels 'hung up', and doesn't know why; none the less he can
wait, 'I've got time'. So although the primitively blue music is
inarticulate because that's what the song is about, we can see how
the inarticulateness links up with the themes of the other songs:
and directly with the two songs that follow, concluding the disc.

Got to get you into my life is again a lyrical McCartney number
that does precisely what George says he can't do. Again it's a
bluesy piece in boogie rhythm, but its melody is heart-easingly
songful, beginning with an upward leaping sixth which then
grows to an octave, and ending its first strain with a prancing
seventh. He was alone, he says, took a ride, and found 'another
kind of mind there', the whole of this opening clause bouncing
over a tonic pedal, sometimes with flattened seventh. In the
second strain he 'suddenly sees' her: the bass descends chromatically, creating relatively rich harmonic movement after the
static opening: whilst the springing melody is subtly syncopated
across the beat. The exclamatory OOOH when he sees her is
almost comic, yet magical, too. The middle section is instrumental

Ex. 28

Then I sud — — den-ly see —— you   ooh—

except for a falsetto cry on a false related B flat ('Got to get you into my life'). If it sounds a little desperate, the return of the lyrical tune appears, in context, the more confident. The song doesn't, however, end but fades out: which may indicate that the Beatles no longer see the love relationship as an easy answer. The extraordinary concluding song, *Tomorrow never knows*, in any case encourages us to 'turn off your mind, relax and float downstream', taking up the theme of John's dream song and giving it metaphysical formulation. Drums and a tambura drone on C re-establish an oriental atmosphere, while the melody alternates a non-metrical phrase on the triad of C major with a triplet on the fifth, rising to the flat seventh, then to the tonic. 'It is not dying, it is shining, it is the end of the beginning' we're told, with sundry references to the Tibetan *Book of the Dead* culled from Timothy Leary. But if this is the first significant narcotics song, it is so as consummation of themes we have seen to be implicit throughout. Far from being Brummagen (or Liverpudlian) orientalism, it's a logical and uncompromising evolution from quintessential Beatleism; indeed, its pentatonic refrain is identical with that of the very first song (*I saw her standing there*) on which we commented. It's significant that the song is John's, not

Ex. 29

George's, though John is the iconoclast whereas George had become identified with the religious, or quasi-religious, elements in Beatle music. Moreover, the singing voice, which is here the mind alone, is gradually engulfed in an electronic hubbub emulating the cries of birds and beasts, the hurly-burly of the natural world. Having begun with adolescent regression, the Beatles conclude the first work of their young maturity with an almost-literal aural synonym for return to the womb. There are parallels to this in avant-garde jazz (the jungle noises possibly derive from Mingus) as well as in 'art' music, but this doesn't weaken the impact of the song, even after half a dozen years and a multiplicity of imitations. No further testimony to the authenticity of Beatle music is needed.

Revolver contains the first specifically hallucinatory Beatle song. The two singles they next issued – Paul's *Penny Lane* and John's *Strawberry fields forever* – both relate the LSD experience to childhood memory and a *new* Eden discovered within the mind; both, if they can hardly 'justify' the drug experience, demonstrate its relevance to the Beatles' development. Penny Lane is a real place, a bus roundabout in Liverpool, and the barber, the banker, the fireman, the children who figure in it are at once revocations of the Beatles' own childhood and mythic figures from a children's comic. It really is 'very strange' that the banker 'never wears a mac in the pouring rain'; and the fireman who likes to keep his 'clean machine' clean is at once real and surreal: as indeed is the whole streetscape 'in my ears and in my eyes, there beneath the blue suburban skies'.* There's a deeply mysterious poetry of the commonplace here: which naturally finds reflection in the music. The tune begins, almost like a kids' street jingle, in a simple B flat major, rising-falling scale; but the first clause ends with a D flat triad telescoped over the B flat tonic as bass, and the second strain finds its way to the flat submediant, stopping to 'say hello' in a B flat minor cadence which concludes, however, not with the tonic but the dominant. Moreover, although there are the conventional eight bars in the verse, they're oddly divided as four plus three plus one, and the refrain ('Penny Lane is in my ears and in my eyes') is in A flat major, having used the subdominant of B flat as its pivoting dominant. The return for the next stanza is made by way of an abrupt dominant seventh

---

* This is what Paul sings, though the organ version has the more Edenic '*wet* beneath the skies . . .'

on the curious word 'meanwhile', which deliberately muddles both syntax and chronology. So for both musical and verbal

Ex. 30

reasons the song comes out as childishly merry yet dreamily wild at the same time. The hallucinatory feeling concerns problems of identity rather than drugs specifically, asking what, among our childhood memories, is reality and what is illusion; as the charming words put it:

> *A pretty nurse is selling poppies from a tray,*
> *And though she feels as if she's in a play,*
> *She is anyway.*

We're all involved in this play when a high trumpet crazily intrudes in double track technique. The effect recalls Charles Ives' multi-orchestral pieces, though it's improbable that, at that date, the Beatles knew much of Ives' music. The trumpet interlude is brilliantly played (by Philip Jones); yet its wit and fancy both reveal and enhance the quintessential Beatleism of the song, which has no end, but merely ceases on the subdominant.

This is a most beautiful, strange, and 'achieved' piece of oral poetry become music, still innocent, yet remote from the Beatles' boyish initiation a brief five years earlier. The same is true of the companion song, *Strawberry fields forever:* which also refers to a real place, for Strawberry Fields was a Salvation Army School where John, as a child, was taken by Aunt Mimi to the annual fête and garden party, chuffled ice cream, and was enraptured by the Salvation Army band. Here, however, it's the evocative name itself that triggers off the song rather than memories of a childhood past; and whether or no because it's directly concerned with taking a trip, it's certainly the strangest Beatle song thus far, no longer discussable within the frame of pop convention. John's taking us down to Strawberry Fields where 'nothing is real' and 'living is easy with eyes closed'. The words get gradually less intelligible, more maudlin, with each stanza, and though the music doesn't change, its interpretation does. To begin with, it's odd enough. The first section has nine bars, divided with an irregularity convincing because it's an extension of the verbal rhythm. The dreamful descent to Strawberry Fields is accomplished by a lunge, with sickening instrumental glissando, to a flattened dominant seventh: succeeded on 'nothing is real' by a cavernous dominant ninth of B minor which, after hazy vacillation, resolves or fails to resolve into the tonic A major in an irregular 6/8 rhythm and drooping appoggiatura (see Ex. 31). The 'middle' has two four-bar phrases; but the hallucinatory atmosphere is maintained through the vaguely shifting rhythms (crotchet triplets, quavers, semi-quavers) of the monotone vocal line, mumbling to itself – 'I think I know I mean,* ah, yes, but it's all wrong' – as it sinks below consciousness. Perhaps the rhythmic and tonal freedom and the linear flexibility or slackness prove darkly liberating, for the original fragmentary tune, on its return, survives the sinister distortions of the instrumental sonorities. The lyricism doesn't, however, survive the jibbering electronic freak-out at the end. That would seem a total abdication of human volition, to go on from which necessitated a radical

* A variant reading (organ version) is 'I think I know *of thee*'.

reorientation. The Beatles were equal to it: and produced *Sgt. Pepper's Lonely Hearts Club Band,* the single most decisive event in pop's brief history.

Ex. 31

4. Sgt. Pepper and the Lonely Hearts

We have seen how Beatle music began as a communal activity of danced song: and how in their second phase – as verbal developed alongside musical interest – it became concerned with human relationships in a social context. The songs were now to be listened to, rather than danced to; and by the time of *Penny Lane* and *Strawberry fields* it was improbable that the numbers could even be 'participated in' in live performance, since they were dependent on electronic equipment. This does not necessarily mean that the songs have ceased to have ritual significance, for the long-playing record is a more radical innovation than we once realised. It transplants ritual from temple or theatre into any place where two or three may gather together, including the home or commune, as well as club or discotheque. This is why the supreme achievements of pop so far are halfway between ritual and art. With remarkable verbal articulateness, though at a poetic level beyond intellectual formulation, the Beatles' next disc, *Sgt. Pepper's Lonely Hearts Club Band*, explores the perennial as well as current problems of adolescence – loneliness, friendship, sex, the generation gap, alienation, fear, nightmare; and perhaps could do so because the Beatles' early 'corporate identity' was always a synthesis of four separate individualities. Yet if *Pepper* is, in this relatively traditional sense, art, it is also a ritual involving the young – through its electronic extension of musical sounds into the environment of the external world – in a ceremonial togetherness, without the prop of church or state. This two-way function as art and ritual remains valid, even though the Beatles, in common with most pop groups, disclaim both moral responsibility and artistic technique: for that responsibility and technique may be intuitively independent of conscious volition is the heart of the matter.

No longer do the Beatles offer us a miscellany of songs; we rather have a sequence of intricately related numbers, forming a whole and performed without break. The verses, though still composed 'orally', by trial and error, are printed on the record sleeve, so that we may go back and read them again, 'like a book': just as on disc we may repeat bits of the music, as one cannot in a live (especially in part improvised) performance. None of the songs is a love song; and that the main theme of the sequence is loneliness would seem to admit that the Beatles' early attempts at tribal togetherness had failed – not as music, but as a way of life. *Sgt. Pepper* himself is an old-world character rooted in the camaraderie of a distant past: 'It was 20 years ago today Sgt. Pepper taught the band to play.' So we open with a 'public' number (by Paul), inviting us to the show, and recalling Edwardian military music, the circus and the working man's club, delivered with extrovert rhetoric, and with approving audience noises off stage. Yet if the brisk rhythm, the jaunty fanfares and the military scoring of this first song suggest simple solidarity, the music is far from being what it superficially seems. In tonality it is curiously ambiguous: for while it gravitates towards a smiling G major, the introduction wobbles between dominant sevenths of D and F, and when we reach the tune itself and the Band, having been introduced, plays and sings, the rhythms of the tootling arpeggiated tune are tipsily displaced by cross accents (three against two) and the 'open' tonality is clouded by blue false relations (see Ex. 32). So this public show-piece hides beneath its zest a certain jitteriness. The cosy world of Pepper may embody a truth; but it's one that is dubiously relevant to the young today. On the cut-out included with the disc the Beatles sport their resplendent Edwardian uniforms as comic fancy-dress.

Indeed, the instability in this first song already demonstrates that although Pepper is a military man, very peppery, and runs a band of people playing *together*, they none the less play to a club of Lonely Hearts. So we're not surprised when the public junketings fade out, after a reference to the 'lovely audience' Pepper hopes we're going to be, into a sad little song, also by Paul with help from John, but sung by Ringo, commonest of common men. And he begins by apologising for his incompetence, as contrasted with peppery professionalism. What would we say

Ex. 32

We're Ser-geant Pep-per's lone - ly hearts — club band — We

hope you will en-joy the show—

if he 'sang out of tune' or 'out of key': with the imputation that he
probably will, for he once confessed 'I'm not very good at singing
because I haven't got a great range. So they write songs for me
that are pretty low and not too hard'. Then he goes on to say that
he thinks he'll get by with '*A little help from my friends*'. He's
the least talented, the least articulate, 'inferior' member of the
group; none the less he has his own unassailable identity: which
will be enough, given a modicum of love. 'What do you see when
you turn out the light? I can't tell you, but I know it's mine':
so the minor miracle of the song is that it means precisely what it
says. While taking over from *Sgt. Pepper* the manner of the
old-fashioned music hall, it creates a childishly simple, narrow-
ranged, repetitive tune that has the *pristine* quality of the earliest
Beatle songs. The difference is that Ringo now knows he's small
and (almost but not quite) alone. There's a painful suspended
(sharp) seventh on the phrase 'Do you need anybody'; the song
epitomises the reasons why the Beatles needed one another and
reveals why their awareness of 'separateness' and 'togetherness'
was meaningful to the young at large.

It has been suggested (by, among others, Spiro Agnew!) that *A little help from my friends* implies a reference to drugs: which seems totally irrelevant to the disarmingly basic theme of the song, in which the language is plainly Ringoesque. The next song, *Lucy in the sky with diamonds*, is by John and is pretty generally described as an LSD song, because its title spells it, and because its unplain, highly coloured, 'psychedelic' imagery is comparable with that of *Penny Lane* and *Strawberry fields forever*. John denies this; certainly the song makes better sense as a revocation of a dream-world of childhood, triggered off by a drawing of a schoolmate by John's son, Julian. If the lovely opening lines – 'Picture yourself in a boat on a river With tangerine trees and marmalade skies' – recall the imagery of Bob Dylan's hallucinatory songs, they also evoke a childhood world quintessentially Beatle-like, and the vivid colours are those of a poetically recreated kids' comic. The music, too, preserves its innocence: a lazily wafting waltz tune undulates around the third of the scale (with dreamy flat sixths and sevenths in the accompaniment), and the fairy-tale scoring, tinklingly plangent, helps us to see and hear the lovely landscape as larger than life, the flowers 'incredibly high', the girl's eyes 'kaleidoscopic'. The vague tonality, shifting from a modal A up to B flat, helps to float us away on the water, in our 'newspaper taxi', looking for 'the girl with the sun in her eyes' (see Ex. 33); at which point the Beatles characteristically bring us back to earth with an abrupt change from slow waltz time to a rapid 4/4. The refrain yells, in hammering repeated notes, Lucy (whose name means light) in the sky with diamonds, in what looks like G major, counteracting the B flat key signature, but is perhaps a plagal approach to the triad on D, a magic talismantic *Ah*, highly equivocal in effect. The re-statement of this brusque refrain as coda acquires three sharps as key signature, though the G sharp never appears, no more than in the original waltz. This time the D major triad forms a plagal cadence to A, but without any sense of finality; and the fade-out carries us back from trip, childhood and dream-girl to reality, though again with equivocal irony.

Getting better is a raggy music-hall song by Paul, evoking school rebel and angry young man. The scalewise-moving, non-

Ex. 33

slow-ly   a girl with kal - eid - o-scope   eyes.____
flow-ers   that grow so in - cred - i - bly   high.____
turn-stile   the girl with kal - eid - o-scope   eyes.____

Cel - lo-phane flow-ers of   yel-low and
News-pa-per tax - is   ap - pear on the

modulating, boogie-rhythmed tune expresses fury with rule and
authority and lovelessness in personal relationships, with perky
insouciance; while the refrain tells us that since he's met 'her',
he's been getting better all the time. Though the language is not
only plain, but blunt, the music doesn't allow us to take the self-
denunciation, or even the denunciation of authority, very seriously.
At the same time the diatonic simplicity of the refrain makes its
optimism somewhat wobbly. This again indicates how the
Beatles' vulnerability is part of their honesty; so it's natural
enough that this emotional frailty should lead into the deepening
'commitment' of the next song, *Fixing a hole*, which is also
Paul's. We've moved from Sgt. Pepper's old-world club to the
dubious potentiality of friendship; from there to a dream-girl or
the fairy-world of childhood; from the dream-girl to a remotely
possible real one; and from that nervous expectancy to this
subtly mysterious little song about the nature of identity. He's
fixing the holes, papering over the cracks, in the shell that protects

him in order that his mind may 'wander where it will go': so what looks like imprisonment is really freedom. The words function like runic poetry, reverberant though not intellectually formalised; in being self-reliant, the lyrical McCartney tune is the first melody in the sequence of songs to stand – or rather to lilt – on its own feet, insidiously haunting, virtually free of the usual influences, black or white. It begins in a dorian F, rocking fourths being followed by a pentatonic upward lift, balanced by a descending flat seventh; the end of the first strain creates the mind's free wandering, as it floats pentatonically upwards, always just off the beat. The middle section tells us that, thus freed,

Ex. 34

he's 'right where I belong', the lyricism changing to diatonic F major with sharp sevenths and high tessitura, as he refers to the people outside who cannot get into (and perhaps threaten) his private world. But the lovely, lilting dorian tune returns, to fade out in timeless pentatonic melismata.

Being concerned with me-in-myself, this song can provide a transition to the next, which is about the most deeply rooted of ties, those of family. *She's leaving home* is also by Paul, though John wrote some of the words. The girl and her situation, though typical enough, were culled (Paul tells us) from the *Daily Mirror*, and the verses evoke the mystery of the commonplace, having the true economy of poetry. How much is conveyed by the reference to the 'note that she hoped would say more'; how sadly funny it is that she leaves home for the purpose of 'meeting a man from the motor trade', probably a shady rather than conventional character, but either way one from whose life-style the glamour will soon wear thin. Even the parents' lamentation ('With never a thought for ourselves . . . we gave her everything money could buy'), though guyed with falsetto obbligato, is without trace of bitterness.

The musical structure, whether or no it's empirical, is both irregular and subtle. We begin with a four-bar instrumental introduction over a tonic E major triad, with romantically plashing harp. The vocal tune is a corny waltz mainly in stepwise movement, but with a yearning lift from the second to the tonic in the higher octave, followed by a descent by way of the flattened seventh. This first phrase runs to five bars, rounded off by an instrumental ritornello of three bars with emotive solo cello apparently modulating to the dominant. But the next phrase of the tune reasserts the tonic; and what looks like a repeat of a four-bar phrase is extended to nine bars, with a postlude of another three bars solo cello, again modulating to the dominant. Once more the modulation is frustrated; and the verse section is completed with a four-bar phrase in the tonic, repeated. The chorus or middle – the conventional terminology hardly applies – has the falsetto obbligato for the parents; but their vocal line overlaps with that of the narrator of the girl's story, so the nineteen bars of music don't establish any regular periodicity in phrasing. Both the asymmetrical phrasing of the tune or tunes and the repeated frustration of the modulation sharpwards keep us on tenterhooks; even the extended passage of dominant sevenths of the dominant in the coda doesn't resolve on to the tonic but relapses to a *sub*dominant A major triad, which then forms a plagal (Amen) cadence back to E. This happens on the exclamation 'Bye-bye', which puns on 'getting by' and 'money can buy' in the previous stanzas: an effect quaintly comic and clownishly sad.

Ex. 35

Throughout, the song, though parodistic, is never destructive. The arching cello tune is as beautiful as it is comic; and the irregular structure *enacts* the story, conveying not merely the fact of the girl's departure but all the muddled hope, apprehension and fear in the girl's heart, the fuddled incomprehension of the parents. There's failure all round, in both generations; yet the failure doesn't deny the tune's heart-felt lyricism, nor lessen the comedy of the falsetto obbligato. That the song makes us laugh and cry simultaneously is testimony to its truth to experience.

This little tragi-comedy of personal relationships is banished with a return to the public world of the circus (this time evoked by John), *Being for the benefit of Mr. Kite*, the words of which arc in fact taken from an old circus poster. The public world seems, again, to be one of mindless merriment, though tonally it is as disquieting as *Sgt. Pepper*, with comparably falling sequences undermining the antics on the trampoline. The song's function in the cycle is more important than its intrinsic interest; it recalls our starting point, after the songs have explored the ramifications of loneliness and togetherness; and by ironic contrast it prepares the way for George Harrison's number *Within you without you*, which opens the second side. This brings in the religious implications of the search for identity. 'The space between us all' – which was the burden of most of the songs on side 1 – will be abolished when we submit to love, and 'life flows on', within us and without us. The Indian drone of eternity returns, and George's sitar playing attains some complexity. Of course it doesn't rival, or even seriously emulate, the 'real right thing', for the orientalism is re-created in terms of the Beatles' newborn innocence. The rocking fourths and flattened sevenths have a significant affinity with those of that quintessential Beatle tune, *Fixing a hole*, which is also concerned with identity (see Ex. 36); but in Harrison's song the freeing of the mind literally breaks the time-barrier, so that the metres shift, over the endless drone, between fours, fives and threes. Wailing microtonal intervals are employed in a 5/8 instrumental interlude.

From these metaphysical reaches within the mind we're jerked back by a leery laugh: a deliberate exercise in 'trivialisation' which may be self-defensive, though it's not self-destructive. For the next song, Paul's *When I'm sixty-four*, cannot be adequately described as parody, though we're back in a suburban terraced house, and in the raggy, twentyish music-hall style of George Formby, with oompahing tuba bass and noodling clarinet obbligato. This reinvokes Dad's world and era with comic yet touchingly poetic wit. Again it's the selectivity in the use of commonplace detail that counts, as in such funny but deeply reverberating phrases as 'I could be handy mending a fuse When

Ex. 36

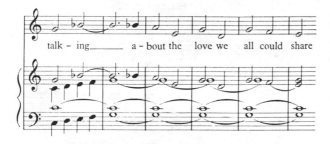

your lights have gone'; of course the oldies' little cottage (if they can afford it) has to be in the Isle of Wight, and of course their grandchildren must be called Vera, Chuck and Dave (these names were supplied by John). Yet these oldies are at the same time identified with the Beatles; and the last stanza shifts from old-time music-hall to the commercialised present of Mr. Lonelihearts – 'send me a postcard, drop me a line, Stating point of view, Indicate precisely what you mean to say Yours sincerely, wasting away'. Chronology is fuddled, and it's the oldies, the Beatles, and we ourselves who are wasting away; when the verse says, 'give me your answer Fill in a form, Mine for evermore' we realise how pitifully frail are human institutions and resolutions, opposed to the thud of Time. So the refrain 'Will you still need me, will you still feed me, When I'm sixty-four' comes out as characteristically vulnerable in its funniness; there's even a hint that, when that distant day comes, my music may sound as corny as this. Only it isn't, in fact, corny at all, since the old-fashioned ragtime is as marvellously recreated as are the words. To begin with, there's a touching contrast between the first

phrase, naïvely pentatonic despite the chromatic passing note, and
the piquant rising and falling chromatics of the second phrase:
while the middle section – minor thirds for the cottage in the
Isle of Wight, sustained minims arching up to a high G for the
recognition that 'you'll be older too' – reveals a pathos that is
disturbing as well as wistful. When the infectiously catchy tune

Ex. 37

returns we realise that its wit – despite the devastating accuracy
of the words – is benign rather than bitter.

It would seem that the metaphysical exploration of *Within you
without you* has induced rebirth, as did the comparably runic
Tomorrow never knows on *Revolver*. For *When I'm sixty-four*,
though still lonely-hearted, asks whether love can withstand Time,
which is a metaphysical question; and on the whole – despite
those ambivalent ho's and hum's – gives a positive answer. And
if we come back to the present in the next song, Paul's *Lovely
Rita, the meter maid*, it's without illusion. For although lovely

Rita is a girl to balance Lucy in the sky, she's very much on earth, whether in the garage or on the sofa ('with a sister or two'). We're told, though not by Paul, that she's modelled on a Liverpool whore, which hardly fits the verses. Certainly she's for real and, like most people, equivocal. 'The bag across her shoulder made her look like a military man': a fact which relates her to the apparent simplicities of dear old Sgt. Pepper, and which makes the genteel invitation to tea – it *is* tea, not pot, Paul tells us – the more weirdly poetic. Her music, anyway, is brisk, almost perfunctory, despite the pentatonic opening phrase and the romantically echoing sequence a tone lower when first he sees her. She's a good-time girl who doesn't need or get emotional commitment; this makes for happiness of a kind, exuberantly expressed in a barrelhouse instrumental interlude. But the song doesn't pretend that lovely Rita is more than an alleviation of loneliness and distress, and the pantings and motor noises which the number ends with or peters into carry an indefinite threat. Something of this persists through John's *Good morning* song, which is ostensibly a paean for created Nature wherein beating Beatles are joined by crowing roosters, barking dogs, mewling cats and chirruping birds. The delight-giving pentatonic tune tells us that 'I've nothing to say and that's O.K.' Mere being is enough, so the morning is good indeed, and can carry us back to a reprise of Sgt. Pepper's music of social solidarity, with additional brass fanfares, and with applause and laughter off – an effect culled, we are told, from Stockhausen's *Momente*! Yet both the *Good morning* song and the reprise of *Sgt. Pepper* are oddly equivocal in effect. *Good morning*'s euphoria has a spooky, hallucinatory undertone, contrasting cosy tea-time with the Little Wife with the world outside where 'everything is closed, it's like a ruin'; so we're not surprised when the sounds of celebrating creatures merge into ugly and exacerbating street noises. Similarly Sgt. Pepper's number, in its return, has lost its show-biz glamour, or recognises it as illusory. Instead of the former jovial bonhomie, the words reiterate 'Sgt. Pepper's lonely', four times. The noises off are yet more scared and scary than those of *Good morning*: so the triumph for Pepper's hotness is ambiguous, though not double-faced.

This being so, it's logical that the disc shouldn't, after all, end with the reprise. An epilogue is appended, which transports us back into the 'real' world – *A day in the life* of any young, lonely heart. John has told us that this really was a joint composition, 'a peak, a real . . . The way we wrote a lot of the time, you'd write the good bit, the part that was easy, like "I read the news today" or whatever it was, then when you got stuck or whenever it got hard, instead of carrying on you just drop it; then we would meet each other and I would sing half and he would be inspired to write the next bit and vice versa.' The dual authorship perhaps helps give the song its representative quality, whereby it stands for a generation; but John deserves the credit for initiating this deep little song with one of the most haunting phrases in Beatle music: a pentatonic slip of a tune, sounding the more frail in John's guileless presentation, telling us how 'I read the news today, Oh boy!' and though some of it is funny, more of it gives me the creeps (see Ex. 38). The news items mentioned in the poem are authentic; the man who 'blew his mind out in a car' was a friend of the Beatles who killed himself driving a car when on drugs; and this item of personal news is kaleidoscopically fused with the usual scenes of war and violence picked up from a glance at a paper, including such particularly riveting items as the four thousand holes in Blackburn, Lancashire, which is a reference either to the police probes in the Moors murder case or to a local councillor's complaints about the state of the roads – the authorities disagree! Paul, in an interview with Alan Aldridge, has denied most of the personal references, as well as most of the references to drugs in this song and others. Whatever the facts, he's in principle right, for the particular references are not what the songs are about. Indeed, in a sense they confuse rather than clarify; the point about the news items here is that they're a Day in the Life – anyone's life, here and now; and what matters in the touching first section of the song is precisely the contrast between the simplicity and frailty of the little tune and the horror and confusion of the events dispassionately referred to. Significantly, the verse section is without modulation, except in so far as its pentatonic-tending E minor acquires tight, phrygian F

Ex. 38

naturals. It's rejected by a long electronic crescendo ushering in a middle section in a triadically pentatonic E major, the beat grown stronger, the tempo more urgent. Despite the comic pantings and realistic detail ('found my coat and grabbed my hat, made the bus in seconds flat') this middle section (sung by Paul) turns hallucinary, opposing the dream within the mind, whether or not narcotically induced, to the nightmare of the 'news' outside. The final da capo of the original tune is not less lyrical,

Ex. 39

though it's lost its innocence, being threatened by ferocious percussion, and leading into another and wilder electronic trip that seems to be also an atomic explosion, obliterating both public revelry and private love.

So the song comes out as at once richly comic and deeply melancholic, agitating nerves we hardly knew we possessed. It's the Beatles' deepest exploration of their familiar illusion-reality theme; for them 'the tragedy' is simultaneously terrifying (in a personal sense) and grotesque (as an item in a newspaper, with a picture that almost makes you laugh). Most of this is epitomised in John's singing of the sublimely understated phrase 'though the news was rather sad': which doesn't evade any of the horror, but brings us through it with something like a wry smile. Perhaps it's an unconscious tribute to the Beatles' innocent honesty and tough resilience that, after the explosion, the commotion settles into an infinitely protracted if weirdly spaced (with obtrusive thirds) chord of E major: the key which, in the eighteenth century and after, was traditionally associated – though the Beatles cannot have known this – with heaven!

Sgt. Pepper makes the climacteric point in the Beatles' career, their definite breach with the pop music industry, however materially successful the disc – which in its first two weeks sold a million and a half copies in the United States alone – may have been. Henceforth, the world they've created is *sui generis*, bringing its own criteria. The pattern of their young lives seems clear. In their boyhood they discovered a lost Eden, creating a danced music of which the euphoria was valid because newborn. Their first period ends with their hard day's night's discovery of human relationships and responsibilities; and this 'second period' is consummated in *Sgt. Pepper's Lonely Hearts Club Band*. If Pepper, however, is the apotheosis of the second period, he also initiates the third: much in the same way as *A Hard Day's Night* had one foot in the first period, the other in the second. For whereas many songs in *Pepper* are concerned with the young mind and senses in relationship to the external world, others follow *Tomorrow never knows* (from *Revolver*) in re-entering the world of dream. This preoccupation with the life 'within you' is no longer child-like and innocent, for it absorbs the experience of the Beatles' middle years. So their three periods have a genuine analogy with Beethoven's: though this is not to equate their briefly adolescent experience with that of Beethoven's Promethean lifetime!

Before the Beatles launched their third period with their *Magical Mystery Tour*, they issued a single containing two remarkable songs that form an appendix to *Pepper* and a retrospect on their strange lives up to that point. *Baby you're a rich man now* opens with a richly exotic burbling of shawm and other oriental noises, accompanied however by a briskly basic beat. John asks a question – How does it feel to be one of the beautiful people? – in an oddly bleating tone on the verge of falsetto, the phrase rising through decorated arpeggios of dominant and tonic, with an enquiring tied note at the top; he answers, in the rougher and tougher tones of his normal voice, and the questions (What do you want to be? have you travelled far? how often have you been there?) move from the physical to the metaphysical. So at one level we have a simple success song, with a chorus that begins with an infantile crowing of the repeated tonic, given a crazily disturbing lurch to a diminished seventh when the 'rich man' turns out to 'keep all his money in a big brown bag inside a zoo, what a thing to do'; whilst at another level we have a song about problems of identity, felt with devastating acuteness, even anguish, by four lads from Liverpool transported overnight on a magical mystery tour to fame, fabulous fortune, and the omni-present, all-embracing culture of the global village – which gobbles into its maw the musics of oriental peoples along with Europe's 'concert' music, *kitsch*, American hymnody and jazz, not to mention the oh-so-innocent rock and beat the Beatles had started from. Of course the drug experience is involved also; he's 'travelled far, as far as the eye can see', and the 'beautiful people' are not merely the rich, but also the narcotically initiated. In this sense the electrophonic collage of sounds and musics Eastern and Western is hallucinatory, as it is in some of the songs on *Revolver* and *Pepper*. Yet this only demonstrates that the drug theme exists *because* of the search for identity; drugs or no drugs, this extra-ordinary song makes sense in terms of the Beatles' experience. And although the experience is itself extraordinary it's also deeply relevant to us all, and to the young especially, in a traumatically changing world.

The song on the other side of this single, *All you need is love*, forms a companion piece with *Baby, you're a rich man now*, as did *Strawberry fields* with *Penny Lane*. The material of the song itself could hardly be more basic, for the refrain-introduction begins with the Three Blind Mice descending third, and har-monically oscillates between tonic triads and dominant sevenths – the harmonic norms of Western 'progress' – with mediant triads as link. The middle has one modulation to the relative minor, a simple procedure familiar in conventional classical music as a means of enhancing excitement. Yet this childish rock song isn't what in fact we hear: for the hymnic chanting of the Love Love, Love refrain to the Three Blind Mice motive is itself disrupted in rhythm, a beat dropping out intermittently (or one could think of it as being in 7/4, with an occasional extra beat):

Ex. 40

Love love love love love love

love love love

and it exists only within a collage of love-songs past and present, and not merely sexual love-songs at that, for the first thing we hear is the *Marseillaise*, signifying an overtly ironic love of country. Distant taped murmurs of other songs continue during the cornily yet obsessively reiterated love-chant until, in the coda, the extraneous noises take over, engulfing the chant in snippets of muzak from cocktail lounge or bar, in an ironically nostalgic quotation from *She loves you*, and finally in a dissolving fragment of *Greensleeves*.

While these effects may begin parodistically and include self-parody (which maturer Beatles have always been prone to), the total impact of the song is far from being satirical. On the contrary, it comes out as infinitely sad, reminding us that although man through history has sought for love he's seldom found it: for love of nation or of 'humanity' is illusion, and love of man and woman, parent and child, inevitably temporal and fallible. 'There's nothing you can do that can't be done, nothing you can sing that can't be sung', the words say, spoken against the chanted refrain; and the point of the words lies – another inspired example of oral composition – in their opacity. For though on the surface of the mind one accepts them as meaning that with love one could do anything and everything, what they in fact say is that everything has been done already, and always in vain. So if *All you need is love* is obviously not a simple song of sexual love (as a song with that title would have been in the Beatles' early years), neither is it a happy hippy song telling us that if only we'd all love one another, all would be well. Its hallucinatory qualities turn out to be basic, if not exactly sober, truth. All we *need* is love; and experience suggests that we haven't much hope of finding it. This is the more disquietingly true in the fabulous world in which the Beatles unwittingly find themselves. This disc is made possible only by electronic technology and the multiple media of the global village; and it's this which has transformed the Beatles from ordinary Liverpool lads into extraordinary mythic heroes. Though electronic technology now seems to swallow them whole, their real heroism lies in the fact that they have not been corrupted by their metamorphosis; and because of their incorruptibility they have revealed the real nature of the transmutation of 'electronic age' man. In this sense their total achievement may be more significant than that of many artists and thinkers whose work would conventionally be considered 'great'.

Part Three
Rebirth and
Return of the Initiate

5. A Magical Mystery Tour to Abbey Road

These two related songs – *All you need is love* and *Baby, you're a rich man now* – are concerned, indirectly and intuitively, with the Beatles' historicity – their relationship to their own and to 'civilisation's' past. They needed to create them before they could enter the renewed world of the inner life: as they did in the sequence of dream songs incorporated in their television film, *A Magical Mystery Tour*. The film itself, despite marvellous moments, was hardly a success: though one might excuse its slack self-indulgence on the grounds that the Beatles dispensed with the services of a professional director out of a positive instinct for self-reliance. Whatever one thinks of the film, the songs are splendid; and only one of them – *Your mother should know* – looks back to the Beatles' earlier song types. This number, like most of the nostalgic songs, is by Paul. The words say 'Let's all get up and dance to a song that was a hit before your mother was born, though she was born a long long time ago': so naturally enough it's a ballad-style song, more lyrical than Paul's *When I'm sixty-four*, but with a comparable fusion of wit and nostalgia. Even in this song, however, the lyricism, which relates us to a distant, cosy past, is dreamily mysterious, in an eleven-bar phrase, divided as four plus four plus two plus one. The springing A minor arpeggio dances up to a dissonant seventh; looks as though it's falling to tonic major; which turns out to acquire a flattened seventh, leading us to D minor which then acts as supertonic of C. Yet the C major triad proves to be no conclusion, for it shifts immediately back to a dominant seventh in A, and then falls sequentially to G and C, and so back to the relative A minor for the repeat (see Ex. 41). The middle, mainly in wordless vocalise, wavers between A minor and C major, lyrically nostalgic, not so much for home and the past as for the dream world we're hoping to discover, or rediscover, on our Magical Mystery Tour.

There's a similar quality in the title song, *Magical Mystery Tour*, also by Paul, for though we begin with the circus showman's rhetorical advertisement, like Sgt. Pepper's first song, the invocation itself is magically vague in tonality, telescoping G major and B flat major triads into what turns out to be a basic F major. The audience-noises and trumpet and horn fanfares are also hazier than Pepper's, and the tune's obsession with the flat seventh gives it a folky flavour which is more deeply explored in the other songs. The heart of the matter – and the genesis of the Beatles' third period – is in the complementary songs *The fool on the hill* and *I am the walrus*, the former by Paul, the latter by John. The Fool is an astonishing invention, who justifies the implicit parallel with Blake's holy innocent. His gentle tune, with pastoral recorder obbligato, innocently out of tune, is in D but with a plagal feel; the first strain runs to six bars of stepwise movement with an occasional 'open' fourth and a pentatonic

Ex. 41

melisma on 'fool' at the end. The apparent return to D turns into a *minor* triad – an effect of a solemnity hardly less disturbing than Schubert's typical juxtapositions of major and minor. There's a one-bar transition ('he never gives an answer') to the second, four-bar strain, in which there is no dominant-tonic cadence. Alone on his hill, the Fool watches the sun go down (on a Schubertian flat submediant) and the world spinning round (a tonic minor triad intensified with a dissonant ninth as appoggiatura, which is resolved upwards before sinking to the tonic)

Ex. 42

(see Ex. 42). The last stanza separates the Fool from the worldly others who are the real fools and, of course, identifies him with a Beatle. The identification is justified by the music: which has the haunting simplicity and memorability of a folk song, though it is strictly without precedent, pristine.

I am the walrus evokes the creature who is the fool's negative complement – a grotesque beast who lives beneath the watery depths. The song's poetry is surreal, destroying identity ('I am he as you are he and you are me and we are all together') and summoning a gallimaufry of nastinesses, from 'mister city policeman' and 'texpert smoking chokers' to 'pigs in a sty, yellow matter custard dropping from a dead dog's eye'. The song is a mainly two-tone incantation or spell, gyrating between A major-minor and triads of C, D, E and F, with guggling and gurgling noises from the watery walrus. But the naughty things that bubble up from the depths and make us 'cry' in a false related melisma are inseparable from the Fool's foolish positives; and the Walrus's sub- or unconscious also promotes fertility ('I am the eggman') in upward rising sequences, and seems to be part of the fool-child's mythical English world. The 'middle' about sitting in an English garden, waiting for the sun (or the rain will do, at a pinch) is very strange and very beautiful, with modally related triads in parallel motion, almost like Vaughan Williams (see Ex. 43). The two songs together incarnate – give aural flesh to – a psychological truth. Rebirth means regression, which cannot be partial; to relax our minds and 'float downstream' is to accept whatever flotsam and jetsam the subconscious throws up. Newness entails wholeness, and etymologically to be whole is to be hale, which is to be holy: so the Fool couldn't be holy without the Walrus's obscenities. It's interesting that the George Harrison number, *Blue jay way*, patently recalls *Tomorrow never knows*, the beginning of the Beatles' descent 'below' consciousness. His friends have lost their way in a fog; 'they'll be over soon, they said; now they've lost themselves instead'. There's an Indian drone, as usual on C, and the vocal line incorporates augmented seconds or, more accurately, Indian microtonal intervals, undulating between flat and sharp third, with sharpened fourth (see Ex. 44). The

Ex. 43

Sit - ting in an Eng - lish gar - den wait - ing for the sun —

— If the sun don't come

Ex. 44

Slowly

There's a fog up – on L. A.,

And my friends have lost their way.

middle section asks them to come and join him, faster, but in stepwise moving minims with sharp sevenths grinding against the drone. If they don't come soon, he says, he'll be asleep; and the fade-out perhaps leaves us feeling that there's not much hope of the lost young joining him, and that in any case 'reality' consists, or seems momently to consist, in the Fool-Walrus dream.

So the fog creeps over us. It's still enveloping *Abbey Road* which, if less patently innovatory than *Sgt. Pepper*, is in some ways an even more remarkable disc, since the Beatles, free to follow their fancy, now pursue their Magical Mystery Tour into dangerous as well as mysterious territory.

Thus the first song, John's *Come together*, is one of the strangest – a portrait of a kind of hobo-outcast-messiah, written in juvenile gibberish more scary than comic: which generates a pentatonic line fragmented, jerky, rheumatic in rhythm, with virtually no harmony but with tightly complex percussion. John tells us that it was originally intended as a campaign song for Timothy Leary but turned out differently. Though the effect is distinctly sinister, the walrus-gumbooted holy-rolling point is that we've got to 'come together' to be free; and the screwed up vocal line – squeezed out like a more than usually asthmatic soul singer – attains a near-miraculous release in the refrain, when the reiterated minor third suddenly swings upwards to the fifth, then down to the major third – harmonised, however, with the submediant triad. The soul singer, notably Otis Redding, has clearly

Ex. 45

influenced the vocal style of this record, though as shouters the Beatles don't sound black but rather employ the techniques of ecstasy – pitch distortion and rhythmic ellipses – to reveal the darker depths of their own very English lunacy. Paul's *O darling* might indeed be construed as a parody of Redding, being a wild soul-song in the rhythm and mode of an English folk tune!

Ex. 46

Yet it's typical of the Beatles that the song's passionate intensity is undimmed by the parodistic elements; it's almost a parody soul-song in the same sense as a sixteenth-century parody mass was a serious transmutation of the original. Even in George's *Something*, an apparently straight love song with a soaring tune and richly sequential harmonies, there are intimations of divine fury in the unexpected, 'open' triadic progressions in the cadences, and of near-parody in the soupy strings. Similarly Ringo's *Octopus's garden* is a child's dream-song, hiding something blackly nasty in the woodshed; whilst *Maxwell's silver hammer* is an apparently innocuous, crudely metrical music-hall ditty that is also black comedy in every sense. Paul has said: 'this one epitomises the downfalls in life. Just when everything is going smoothly, bang bang, down comes Maxwell's silver hammer and ruins everything.' But this hardly explains the oddly poetic effect of the murderous narrative, in which the silver hammer is at once weapon for the disposal of bluestocking lovers, school teachers, police and judges, and magic talisman facetiously achieving release. The puerility of the tune is belied by the syncopated oh's and ah's, as well as by the tinkling clink of the silver hammering in the instrumental ritornelli.

Side 1 ends with John's *I want you (she's so heavy)* a song, comparable with, and no less mysterious than, *Come together*. The words of the verse simply tell us that 'I want you so bad, it's driving me mad'; and the post-Pepper music forces us to take the words literally, not as a familiar cliché. Again the tune is as primitively pentatonic as a soul singer's, the vocal production equally wild. Again, there is virtually no harmony: but fierce, even minatory, percussion. The black model is, however, recreated by the Beatles' inspired zaniness; consider the twiddling, flattened melisma on 'want' you. One hesitates to call this effect funny

Ex. 47

though it is nervously hilarious; and this modifies our response to the hammered dominant ninths that instrumentally create his frenzy. With the refrain we discover that being sent mad is, for a third period Beatle, a more frightening process than anything in a soul singer's repertory – unless, perhaps, one harks back to the days of a true primitive like Robert Johnson. For the refrain

consists of a ponderously lurching ostinato in 12/8, apparently in
D minor but with dominant ninths of A (changing to German
sixths on B flat), so that the A major triads are uncertain of their
identity, wobbling between dominants of D and tonics of A. The
words chant 'She's so heavy' in a piercing sonority savagely
amplified. In the coda the chant is repeated remorselessly, with
surging electronic crescendo, until we're on the threshold of a
scream: when it abruptly stops in midstream. In conventional
groove parlance 'heavy' means fine and desirable, so presumably
she is the girl he wants so bad it's driving him mad. Just possibly
she's also heavy simply because she's pregnant and the madness
is that of temporary frustration of desire. This pretty basic
account may indeed fit the facts, for John has said that the song
is about wanting Yoko, and 'she's so heavy' simply means that
she is heavy, though she mayn't look it. Of course, this in no way
discounts the wider and wilder hysteria which the song generates.

Side 2 opens with what seems to be a release from the mad
song's heebie-jeebies. Yet if George's invocation *Here comes the
sun* means what it says in a tune as beguiling as an early Beatle
number, its rumba-like rhythmic contradictions (three plus three
plus two eight) and its occasional harmonic surprises absorb
something of the Beatles' peppery maturity. It's not, therefore,
uncomfortably disturbing when the sun-song is followed by
Because, one of the most beautiful of all Beatle creations. The
words are simple: a runic poetry which of its nature releases
music; which in this case was inspired by Yoko's playing of the
first movement of the Moonlight Sonata, in the early days of
their acquaintance. The musical events in John's love song don't
occur in the same order as in the Moonlight (he says it's the
Moonlight Sonata backwards, though I don't hear that); none
the less the affinity between the enveloping, arpeggiated C sharp
minor triads, with the sudden shift to the flat supertonic, is, in
the Lennon and Beethoven examples, unmistakable. At first the
minor triad arpeggios appear in plangent country guitar style,
reverberantly amplified. The eight-bar first strain rocks slowly in
dotted rhythm through its minor triad ('Because the world is
round it turns me on'), dropping rather than drooping on to the

subdominant triad, and dreamily fading in a melisma. The effect
of this subdominant is unexpectedly emotive, perhaps because the
triadic harmony has been so static. The answering strain extends
and deepens the feeling, since the melody is protracted into
dotted minims, and instead of the subdominant we have a submediant chord of the ninth, the melisma wafting longer and more
hazily. The resolution of this ninth chord on to the supertonic

Ex. 48

is delayed because we shift abruptly back to C sharp minor for
the second stanza, which tells us that 'because the wind is high
it blows my mind'. When, after the second stanza, the dominant
ninth does resolve on to a D major triad, it's hardly a real modulation establishing a new, and remote, key. Its harmonic function
is 'Neapolitan' but the triad, on the exclamation 'Ah', immediately
pivots back from D not to the dominant, but to F sharp, C sharp's
subdominant. This initiates the middle section which, changing

the subdominant minor to major, creates with inspired simplicity the newness and all-embracingness of love. This middle contains four bars only: after which the enveloping arpeggios return and the haunting melody sings da capo, finally floating away in extended melismata, but without harmonic resolution. Indeed, although that flattened supertonic opens heavenly vistas, the song is virtually without harmonic progression, the only significant dominant-tonic cadence in the piece being the one that returns us to our source, and to the da capo of the melody.

The effect of this song is extraordinarily simple, and simply extraordinary. In part this is attributable to the Beatles' two- or three-part vocal texture, in which the melody note is mysteriously disguised: a technique which occurs in many of their finest songs and which has not been employed, at least with anything approaching this subtlety, by other groups. This melodic ambiguity doesn't confuse, but rather enhances, the sense of wonder the tune generates. In this case, too, the arpeggiated tune is absorbed into an arpeggiated accompaniment which is like a lulling of the cradle or even a swaying of the amniotic waters: in which respect there is a direct parallel with the opening of the Moonlight Sonata, as with the gently arpeggiated figurations in the keyboard writing of Schumann. All these musics create a state of trance, though they have nothing specifically to do with the drug experience – which *A day in the life* had revealed as, for Beatles, necessary but purgatorial. It's rather that John has experienced, and recreates in us, a small mystical experience, simply because 'the sky is blue, AH . . . !' In the coda the upward leaping sixth – traditionally an interval of aspiration – is pentatonically suspended on the word 'because'; indeed the arpeggiated swaying is replaced intermittently by silence – in the use of which the Beatles betray something like genius. Causality is released and there is no before and after: *because* that flat supertonic is a moment of revelation, it needs no resolution.

Paul's *You never give me your money* is, if less haunting, hardly less mysterious. He tells us that it was written during the Beatles' financial disputation with Apple, but it's about failure in communication rather than about money *per se*. It's also about love and freedom; and it's the ironic equivocations between the two themes that create the mysterious quality to which I referred. The slowish verse section, veering between tonic minor and its relative major, is nervously stilted, with regularly articulated repeated notes culminating in dissonant appoggiaturas. The musical gaucherie reflects the words, in which long, formal terms like 'negotiations' and 'investigations' preface a metrically syncopated 'break down'. But the second strain, beginning in the relative major and swinging back to tonic minor, is in double time, with rowdy barrelhouse piano, and effects a potent release. So instead of the conventional da capo we return to the original tempo but to a new tune, in rumba rhythm, wobbling between relative major and its flattened seventh: an effect that indeed creates a 'magic feeling' of having 'nowhere to go'. Nor is that the end. Released, we bounce into another tune, now in the tonic major, with upward sixth. The tune has considerable rhythmic

Ex. 49

One sweet dream

animation and variety, so it encourages us to 'take off' and make a 'sweet dream come true'. It induces freedom, becoming tonally rootless as well as rhythmically exuberant; yet it merges into electronic gibbering and beeping that belies the nursery-rhyme paradise of the words: 'one, two, three, four, five, six, seven, All good children go to heaven.' This trip, however induced, is more scary than ecstatic. The seraphic vision of *Because* was momentary, and the rest of the disc trips away from vision and from *Pepper*'s awareness of human relationships into a magical mystery tour that, if it's a dream, is a bad one, and no escape.

The process is effected by way of a chain of short songs, interlinked and interrelated. At least they seem to be, though the Beatles have characteristically said that they were fragments of unfinished songs strung together because they were too good to lose. Paul's *Sun king* begins with pseudo-Aztec drumming and riffs in a pentatonic E major. There's an abrupt shift to C by way of a dominant eleventh; and a solemn little tune moves from fifth to major seventh to tonic and down to the fifth, undulating upwards, in sustained semibreves, to a submediant A, harmonized with the major triad with flat seventh. Yet 'everybody's happy' in a delight-giving alternation of F major triads with dominant sevenths of G; and the coda swings back to pentatonic E major for a magic intonation, in an invented 'global' language, concluding with a snippet of English ('can eat it carousel'). This cantillation is mostly on A major triads with added sixth; its effect is like a child's rune, and can be so because the Beatles are creatures new-born. It's significantly followed without a break, however, by John's *Mean Mr. Mustard*, who is a child's bogyman as well as a real old man with a nasty sister who never takes him out except to look at the Queen (and then he 'shouts out something obscene'). The brief refrain – which could again be part of a children's round-game – oscillates between E and C major, leading into a plagal cadence approached by way of the flattened seventh.

Polythene Pam – a 'mythical Liverpool scrubber' from John's early youth, reinvoked in broad Liverpool accent – and Paul's *She came in though the bathroom window* are also comically scary portraits, at once within the dream and part of the crazy-kinky scene that passes for today's reality. And the last three links in the chain – which are all Paul's – reveal that the dream the Beatles started from, now that it no longer shies away from our society's neurosis, is indeed not far from nightmare. *Golden slumbers* is, in context, an ironic title to an ironic song. Taking up an early Beatle theme, the words tell us, in innocent modality and to rocking parlour-piano accompaniment, that *once* there was a way back homeward; and Paul did in fact light on the traditional words and tune while 'messing about' with a songbook of his stepsister, Ruth, at his father's house in Cheshire. The harmony of Paul's version, however, wanders bleakly and equivocally between A minor, C major and D minor, concluding with a lyrically pentatonic melisma on the traditional words 'Sleep, pretty darling, do not cry'. An irregular extra half-bar leads to a harmonisation of the word 'cry' with the supertonic triad plus seventh and ninth; which chord does precisely what the words tell it not to! Paul's voice almost collapses into speech on the

Ex. 50

Sleep pret-ty dar — ling do not cry

And I will sing a lul-la-by

tender phrase for 'And I will *sing* a lullaby'; and the *Golden slumbers* refrain, though to the original words and a pentatonic tune, is obsessively anchored on the third, and yelled with raucous ferocity, to a heavy beat .The da capo and the 'do not cry' phrase seem, in context, the more woundingly unavailing.

So we abandon the pretence of golden slumbers and drive into a savage rock number asserting that *Boy, you're gonna carry that weight* (in capitals) a long, long time. The burden to be borne is no longer personal, but is that inherent in living, and especially in being a Beatle, after seven years of stardom. Here the beat is everything, though it's grim rather than – as in early Beatle songs – joyous. The tune thrusts manfully up the diatonic scale, only to tumble as we feel the burden of the weight; this time, innocence undocs us! Similarly, the harmony is all 'Western' dominants and tonics, the aggression of which serves only to imprison us. The middle section deals explicitly with the break-down of relationships, 'I only send you my invitations, and in the middle of the celebrations I break down.' The formal 'social' words are precisely articulated as they are in *You never give me your money*, the tune of which is quoted. They sound both blundering and phoney: until breakdown in fact occurs by way of a frigid cross rhythm and the only modulation (to the relative minor) in the number. The dominants and tonics sound yet more remorseless when we hear them da capo, though the final cadence is unexpectedly A major, brusquely syncopated. This is indeed an End – to love, to business dealings, to Beatle-kinship; and the final song – or rather number, since for most of the time the voice is silenced – is a death-knell.

The end begins with an exclamation – 'Oh yeah, ALL RIGHT' – taking us back to the Beatles' wide-eyed boyhood: followed by a question 'Are you going to be in my dreams tonight?' The exclamation is in D major, rising abruptly to the dominant of the dominant, savagely scored, for the question. So the minimal words cover the mindless euphoria of the Beatles' initiation, the love-relationships of their middle phase, and the inner dream of their later days; and leave all suspended on a question mark, to which there is no verbal answer. Perhaps it's interesting that the musical development in *Abbey Road* goes along with a partial relinquishment of the verbal, poetic life progressively explored in *Rubber Soul*, *Revolver* and *Sgt. Pepper*. The verses in *Abbey Road* are certainly more runic, more oral, less concerned with human relationships, though the unconscious springs touched on are now far from being Edenic. This last number, having asked its question, abandons words for a furious hammering of percussion: which leads into a long instrumental section, all dominant sevenths in rumba rhythm, but rocking a tone lower than the starting point, getting nowhere. Suddenly the hubbub stops; there's a tinkling of A major triads on a tinny piano; and Paul's voice returns to sing 'in the end the love you take is equal to the love you make'. The phrase descends scale-wise, harmonised in parallel triads that fall from F major, to E minor, to D minor, to A minor, and so to C major. The final peroration, balancing the fall with rising triads over a deep tonic pedal, is rather grand and not, musically, ironic:

There's plenty of irony in the situation, however, and the last words of the disc are no platitudinous moral aphorism, but a stern *memento mori*. As Paul put it: 'I didn't leave the Beatles. The Beatles have left the Beatles – but no one wants to be the one to say the party's over.'

The end was indeed the end. Except that it isn't, quite: because after a very long silence – during which one might well switch off the record player – we hear a fragment of a tootling, footling George Formbyish ditty telling us that Her Majesty's a very nice girl, oh yeah. *The end's* noble peroration is deliberately trivialised, and the Beatles' funeral is, as George put it, at once 'serious and not serious'.

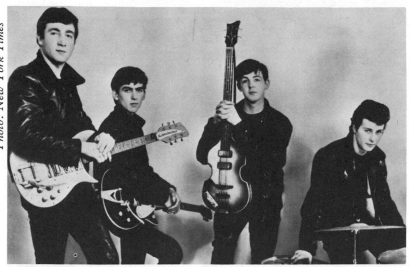

One of the carliest photographs of the Beatles, with, from left to right, John Lennon, George Harrison, Paul McCartney, and Peter Best, . . .

. . . who was later replaced as drummer by Ringo Starr.

The Beatles prepare to invade America in 1964.

A rehearsal for the Ed Sullivan Show in February 1964. On stage, from left to right: Ringo Starr on drums; Paul McCartney and George Harrison at the mid-stage mike; John Lennon downstage and on the TV monitor screen.

The Beatles perform to a huge audience at Shea Stadium, New York, on August 15, 1965.

October 26, 1965: Queen Elizabeth presents the Beatles with Order of the British Empire Medals, which they here display.

Photo: Associated Press

1967: the Beatles arrive in Bangor, Wales, to study the techniques of transcendental meditation with Maharishi Mahesh Yogi, founder of the International Meditation Society.

Photo: Keystone Press

The Beatles pose for a group portrait just prior to the release of *Strawberry Fields Forever*.

Photo: Keystone Press

Paul McCartney, Ringo Starr, John Lennon, and George Harrison in May 1967.

John Lennon (left) and Paul McCartney hold a press conference in New York in May 1968, to discuss the group's latest ventures.

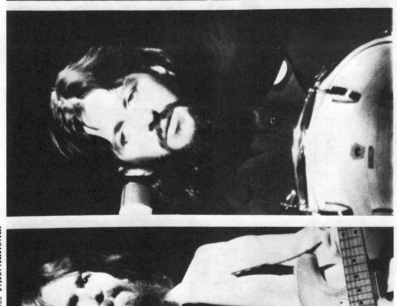

August 1, 1971: ex-Beatle George Harrison and ex-Beatle Ringo Starr perform to crowd of 20,000 people at Madison Square Garden, together with Bob Dylan, in a benefit performance for East Pakistani civil war refugees.

Revolver, *Sgt. Pepper* and *Abbey Road* are the three great milestones in the Beatles' career: *Revolver* because it was a breakthrough from the world of pop into a world that hasn't yet been categorised; *Pepper* because it's the most comprehensively realised Beatle testament; *Abbey Road* because it's their most dangerous adventure. It may be that the personal-cum-mythical statement they made in *Sgt. Pepper* couldn't, once made, be repeated; nor could they have strayed further down Abbey Road without surrendering their 'corporate identity', becoming a different kind of phenomenon. In effect, this is what happened; after *The end* of *Abbey Road* the Beatles pursued separate paths. This is true even though *Abbey Road* was not in fact the last 'corporate' disc the Beatles issued: for *Let it Be* is a deliberate reversal to earlier manners and to a considerable extent consists of earlier – sometimes very early – material. I will discuss this along with the double or White Album, austerely titled *The Beatles*, which appeared after the *Magical Mystery Tour* but before *Abbey Road*, thereby disrupting the evolution of the 'third period'. It is, however, legitimate to relate the *White Album*, as an aftermath, to *Let it Be*, in that it is retrospective in the same sense, if on a larger scale, as were the companion songs *Baby, you're a rich man now* and *All you need is love*. It looks back, with remarkable richness of invention and variety of mood, on the Beatles' career; and submits almost all their own and other peoples' song-modes to the kind of serious parody at which we've seen them to be adept. Though this doesn't necessarily lessen the commitment of individual songs, the consistency of the parodistic approach implies a rejection of the past: which perhaps was necessary before the *Magical Mystery Tour* could find its consummatory way into *Abbey Road*.

The parody works, of course, at various levels, and on the whole is the less interesting the more explicit it is; Paul's *Why don't we do it in the road* is devastingly funny spoof of gutsy R & B (Muddy Waters or Jimi Hendrix) but not much more. Then there's a group of wild rock songs which sound parodistic largely through being so rudimentary. At this stage in the Beatles' career *Birthday* (a joint composition) is a rock song so mindless in its chugging vacuity that it can only sound like self-parody; the quick, pounding rhythm and the mediant transitions are grotesque, but neither ecstatic nor scary. Paul's *Helter skelter* is comparable, rock frenzy being literally 'taken off' on the helter skelter. Other rock songs use familiar techniques of early Beatle music, especially side-stepping modulations, but equivocate by way of texts that are compromisingly ironic. *Back in the U.S.S.R.* turns out as a pro-Beatle but anti-U.S.A. *and* anti-U.S.S.R. song, with old-fashioned reminiscences of Chuck Berry and the Beach Boys. Similarly *Revolution 1* is pro-Beatle but anti-revolution as well as anti-Establishment. Of greater musical substance is John's *Yer Blues*, a parody of blues in general and English blues – as typified by John Mayall – in particular. It's written in three time (though the effect is a slow 12/8), with persistently lacerating blue notes; yet the passion is deflated when John screams 'I wanna die *If I ain't dead already*' very high, in almost comic-falsetto (see Ex. 52). Indeed, he ends by telling us he 'feels so suicidal I even hate my rock and roll': so the parody, despite its exuberance, is self-destructive, and therefore disturbing. In total effect this is a deeply serious song (which John himself thinks well of): one might even regard it as prophetic of the bluesy autobiographical songs in his solo albums.

Parody is less disturbing when the model or victim is the intrinsically less aggressive country music. *The continuing story of Bungalow Bill* stays funny, though it's a total deflation of the tough guy myth. It's a narrative ballad in far-western style with a sting in its tail or tale: 'All the children sing Hey Bungalow Bill What did you kill?' the words being neatly pointed by the tritone in the tune and the flattened subdominant in the harmony. The irony is given an extra twist by the romantic flamenco-style guitar prelude and the lyrical postlude for solo bassoon. Paul's *Rocky Raccoon* is also a Country-Western style narrative ballad that

Ex. 52

wan - na   die___

If   I   ain't dead al - read - y

begins as overt and broad parody. The boogie-rhythmed tune is, however, so infectious that the comic-squalid story is imbued with poetry: and this is still more evident in *Mother Nature's Son*, another McCartney song, which though a satire on Country-Western mythology, is also the song of a Fool on the Hill – not as lyrically touching as the earlier song, but comparable in mood. The descent of the bass line from the B minor triad to G sharp suggests a Foolish wonder, as does the chromatic inner part in the refrain. Yet the satirical element persists, perhaps because of the tune's simple symmetry. Paul's *Blackbird* is a delightful country song contrasting a gently rocking accompaniment with a blue, almost Gospel style melodic riff when the blackbird is advised to fly off 'into the light of the dark black night'. The folk-poetic identification of light and dark in this refrain compli-cates our response to what appears to be a straight little song about freedom, but which turns out to be unexpectedly moving in its fusion of naïve white country guitar with black blues (see Ex. 53). This may be why the squeaky blackbird noises that erupt into the song affect us as being pretty, comic and scary all at

Ex. 53

In - to the light___ of the dark black_ night

the same time. And the blackbirds are followed immediately by
another creature-song, George's *Piggies* who, it seems, are most
people, including you and me; and who sing a corny, metrically
rigid chant accompanied by guzzlings and grunts. The satire is
too simple to be savage, but the song is hardly loving; indeed that
the piggies 'eat their bacon' is a shade horrid.

None the less, the *White Album* contains a high proportion of
love songs, and although most of them embrace irony, few of
them are totally destructive. Paul's *Ob-la-di* is a Liverpudlian-
West Indian music-hall song that deflates love by way of
deliberate vacuity: Molly's answer to Desmond's love is to yell
'ob-la-di, Life goes on' in an upward prancing, Jamaican-style
arpeggio over an oompah bass, but the music's comedy is good-
humoured and rhythmically – if in no other way – enlivening.
Related to Molly is *Martha my dear*, said to be Paul's shaggy dog,
but also a 'silly girl' who won't admit she loves him. The middle
section (or perhaps it's a chorus-refrain) is almost-pentatonic,
almost-falsetto, lilting in or around F but with abrupt changes
of metre and tonality: whilst the verse stutters on a pub piano in
E flat. The irony is still affectionate: as it is in *Honey Pie* who,

though 'a working girl North of England way', has found fame and fortune in the U.S.A. So Paul asks her to come home in a 1930-ish Fred Astaire number. The words are neatly witty, the tune very fetching, so we hope she *does* come home; and the wit of the chromatic harmonies, though nostalgically recalling Rodgers or Cole Porter, preserves a Beatle-like flavour comparable with that of Paul's cabaret-style songs such as *Yesterday* and *Michelle*. The mediant triad on the word 'crazy', and the chromatic slither that ushers in the 'middle' are characteristic touches; and whilst

Ex. 54

Ho-ney Pie,— you are mak-ing me cra — zy,—
Ho-ney Pie,— my po-si — tion is tra — gic,—

the falsetto ah's and ooh's in the coda faintly guy their models, they are true to the Beatles' own world – which has so often managed to be simultaneously innocent and ironic.

John's *Dear Prudence* is a different type of girl, both prudent and virginal, and her number is a new type of Eden song. It's interesting that John, the most 'difficult' and mixed-up Beatle, should also be the one capable of the least equivocal innocence. If in this song there's a slightly satirical flavour about the 'new day-hay-hay' refrain, it's delicately humorous rather than in any sense deflatory. The simple, childhood-evoking lyric invites Prudence 'out to play' in a pentatonic love-call that might be part of a children's game, and the tune is introduced by, and enveloped in, a hazy, countrified sonority pervaded by a tonic E flat pedal, with flattened sevenths dreamily syncopated. There's even a hint – in the subdominant *minor* triads with sharpened seventh that follow the melismatic passages – of the magical solemnity typical of children's round-games (see Ex. 55). John's

Ex. 55

greet the brand new day ha hay   hay ___
see the sun - ny __ ski - hi - hi - - -
like a   lit - tle   ch - hi - hi - - -
greet the brand new day ha hay   hay ___

- - es   The
- - ld   The
                The
                The

Happiness is a warm gun, initiated by an advertisement in an American gun magazine, is parodistic in a much more complex fashion. There are at least three satirical elements – guyings of sophisticated cabaret song, of soul-song-cum-blues, and of corny balladic waltz. Yet the total effect of the song is not satirical but powerfully erotic, and the surrealistic verses would seem prophetically to evoke the darker corners of Abbey Road. Though John is right to protest that the 'gun' has nothing to do with a heroin needle (which scares him) we are not tempted to laugh at the song, even if invited to by the 'bang, bang, shoot' refrain. It's a long way from the virginal sensuality of the Beatles' earliest love songs. There's a similar power to disturb in an ostensibly self-deflating piece like John's *I'm so tired*, in which the title words are so comically yet distressingly enacted by the shift from an A major triad with added second to a triad of G sharp major (see Ex. 56);

Ex. 56

I'm so___ tired   I have-n't slept a wink

and in George's *While my guitar gently weeps* – a song with a line
which, though pentatonic, is remarkably sustained, building to a
powerful climax.

There is no irony in the Harrison number and very little in
Sexy Sadie – except in so far as John says that 'she' is the
Maharishi, the bogus lover every one is waiting for! Even so, the
irony is in the situation, not in the music which, though often
surprising, is too darkly deep to be funny. If we accept Sadie as
a girl, the music presents her as one seriously to be reckoned
with, no doubt because of her sexiness. Her melody is mostly
pentatonic, free in rhythm, with a beautifully seductive balance
to the phrases, the descent through a fifth answered by a rise
through a sixth, then lifted a tone higher, expanding in a melisma
on the high A and G, and tumbling to the original phrase and
pitch (see Ex. 57). She-he 'makes a fool of everyone' by side-
stepping from G major to B minor, and then down a tone to F
natural; her being 'the greatest' is pointed by a piercing chromatic
descent from A to A flat to G. The beat hammers (in quavers)
with persistence and power, if without elation. This girl (or guru)
is an obsession.

So in a very different way is *Julia*, whose song is the only
number in the *White Album* entirely devoid of irony. Julia was
the name of John's mother, who was killed in a car accident when
he was seventeen; if the song is addressed to her, this helps to
explain its mythical-magical intensity, which relates it to John's
love song to Yoko, *Because*, on the later *Abbey Road*. John tells
us, in a repeated note incantation, that 'half of what I say is
meaningless' and then evokes through music a language that is

Ex. 57

deeper than words. The rhythm binds us in a tide-like pulse, with a tremor of agitation created by rumba-like syncopation. The tune, restricted in compass, undulates around A and B, whilst the bass rocks in slow fourths between D and A, B (overlaying the D major triad) and F sharp. The indrawn, contemplative melody suggests mysterious shifts in the harmony (D to B minor 7 to A minor to A minor 9 to B major to G 9 to G minor 7 that might be B flat, and back to D); and there's a characteristic 'modal' swaying between tonic and mediant minor triad (see Ex. 58). The lovely words ('Sleeping sand and silent cloud touch me So I sing a song of love to Julia') thus generate a music of trance which carries us outside Time, comparably with, if less miraculously than, *Because*; and the spell is not broken even by the middle section, wherein her 'hair of floating sky is shimmering, glimmering in the sun' – in the remoteness of C sharp minor with no sharp sevenths. Like Wordsworth's Lucy, she is, in the gently rocking music, 'rolled round in earth's diurnal course With rocks and stones and trees'.

Ex. 58

It is significant that, if *Julia* is addressed to John's mother, it cannot be a simple love-song but must be retrospective, even elegiac, in a deeply serious sense that counterpoints the retrospective parody of most of the other songs. Indeed, the second time the repeated-note chant comes round, the words admit that this love-experience is segregated in a past at once real and mythical: 'When I cannot sing my heart, I can only speak my mind.' So the introverted enclosure of the lyrical impulse in the tranquilly rocking ostinato may be related to the theme of *Glass onion*, which specifically refers back to the Beatles' history. 'I told you about Strawberry Fields, You know the place where nothing is real! I told you about the Walrus and me, I told you about the Fool on the Hill,' John says; and then seems, looking through a glass onion, to dismiss this private mythology in encouraging us to 'see how the other half lives'. Paul had told us, in *Sgt. Pepper*, that he was fixing a hole in order to be alone with and in his mind; *Glass onion* speaks of 'fixing a hole in the ocean', which would seem to be a hopeless undertaking. Relinquishing it seems to produce happiness, though at this stage in the Beatles' evolution one wouldn't expect the joy to be easy. So although *Glass onion* is a fastish, lilting rock number, the tune is obsessed by the disquieting interval of the tritone; the tonality wavers between aeolian A minor and dominant sevenths of B flat (which sometimes sidestep to G minor); and the 'Oh yeah' refrain refers back – with a hint of desperation as well as in parody – to the Beatles' early exclamatory songs.

The backward glance of *Glass onion* is a goodbye, and is the beginning of *The end* that is completed in *Abbey Road*. The *White Album* itself concludes with three connected numbers that also form a goodnight, which is highly equivocal in effect. John's *Cry baby cry* is a permutation or, indeed, an inversion, of a nursery rhyme, the Queen was in the parlour. 'Cry, baby, cry', it says, 'make your mother sigh. She's old enough to know better.' There's hint of domestic dissension; and despite the childish tune, the descending bass line with flattened (phrygian) second grows increasingly threatening until – with the verse about the seance 'in the dark, with voices out of nowhere put on specially by the children for a lark' – the simple ditty becomes a song of revolt. What might be construed as a postlude, the little falsetto refrain 'can you take me back where I come from', in fact turns out to be the back-to-the-womb introduction to *Revolution 9*, an electronic freak-out and collage piece, distorting and mixing muzak of sundry kinds, with conversations and TV statements interspersed. Yoko points out that 9 is the highest number; and the piece spoofs fashionable avant-garderies, the Beatles' own technicians, and implicitly the Beatles themselves, trivialising Sgt. Pepper's electronics as uncompromisingly as *Birthday* or *Everybody's got something to hide except me and my monkey* trivialises the Beatles' earliest rock songs. The overt parody cannot but affect our response to the final *Goodnight* (by John) which opens with the unadulterated adulteration of Hollywooden *schmalz*, all plashing harps and soaring strings. The effect is quite different from the emotive strings in *Yesterday*, *Eleanor Rigby* or *She's leaving home*, for we saw that in those songs the lush accompaniment preserved a virginal frailty that, in context, was at once sentimentally committed and ironically detached. In *Goodnight*, on the other hand, cinematic scoring is unabashed, non-reticent. Yet the words are a child-like lullaby, apparently without irony; the tune, swaying between fourths and fifths, is tenderly beautiful; and the harmonies, telescoping tonics, dominants and subdominants in Ravel-like fashion, are rich without indulgence (see Ex. 59). So there's a delicate balance between the song's intrinsic nature and its self-defensively trivialising treatment; and it won't do merely to say that the sentiment and the satire cancel one another out.

Rumour has it that Vera Lynn, taking the song at its face value, admired and wished to feature it. Certainly it reflects the mythology of her wartime generation: The Girl I left Behind Me, Hearth and Home, What We are Fighting For. Though the Beatles' generation, and their music, have reacted violently against this mythology, which was discredited in the event, there has always been a streak of nostalgia in the Beatles' new mythology. So Vera Lynn's acceptance of the song may not have been entirely wrong-headed, and the parodistic element, though obvious, may be no more than skin-deep. The Beatles' strength has always been

Ex. 59

in their emotional incorruptibility; like Bob Dylan in *Self-Portrait*, they may now be saying that they're incorruptible enough not only to withstand the commercial manipulation of their fabulous lives, but also to redeem the world of commerce which they had cynically celebrated in one of their earliest successes, *Money*. No one would say that Vera Lynn was insincere, any more than were the soldiers whose vicarious sweetheart she was. Sincerity is not enough, but it is a start; and there's a sense in which the Beatles' *Goodnight* reveals the heart's truth hidden beneath that discarded war-time myth. This is why its beauty, despite the cinematic scoring, turns out not to be in inverted commas. The *kitsch* does not discredit the freshness and tenderness of tune and harmony: so the song is reconcilable with the stark nudity of the album's white cover – which served as substitute when naked Beatles were censored.

This is to assume that the Beatles were indirectly responsible for, or approved of, the arrangement of *Goodnight*. At this stage in their career one would think the assumption justified: though Paul does protest that he was appalled by the slushy arrangement of his *The long and winding road*, about which he was not consulted. This song, which was a best-selling single, was included on the Beatles' final disc, *Let it Be*, the music of which is mostly retrospective in mood, seldom overtly parodistic, and – at least as compared with *Abbey Road* – pervasively benign. Whether or no Paul approved of the plush scoring of *The long and winding road*, it works not because it guys the feeling but because the feeling has integrity. The music has a tremulous expectancy, created partly by the delayed appearance of the tonic (though the key is E major, we start with a modal C sharp minor and modulate flatwards to A before cadencing in E); and partly by the tentative contour of the melody, which hovers between fourths and thirds, in gently exploratory rhythms suggested by the words. The

Ex. 60

middle section is purely pentatonic in a triadic E major; so the da capo wistfully disturbs this simplicity as it yearns homeward, from its shiftier tonality, to the light of E – which, incidentally, had been the Eden key for Schubert. A melodic line and tonal evolution as subtle as this cannot be construed ironically, and the sensitivity recreates the cinematic scoring. As in Dylan's *Self-Portrait* again, the song probes to the truth within the Hollywooden myth, and the barrier between 'art' and 'commerce' is revealed as illusory. It's interesting that the scoring of John's *Across the universe* – a countrified version of the Beatles' earlier 'metaphysical' songs – is similarly opulent, yet paradoxically pure in effect. This is an incantatory song with an almost metre-less vocal line floating stepwise over simple triadic harmonies of tonic, dominant, subdominant and mediant, sometimes telescoped and synchronised, occasionally changed to minor. The sonority is

Ex. 61

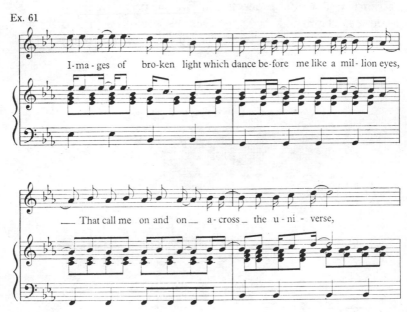

enveloping, the mood hymnic; and there's a magical talismantic refrain 'Jai Guru Deva Om'. Yet the piece is neither oriental nor satirical in manner; the flux of the visible universe – evoked in the beautiful poem – is timelessly stilled in a sublimation of folk and Country-Western music. *Let it be* is also a hymnic song, entirely without modulation, halfway between C major and A aeolian, with pentatonic roulades. Though the words lack the runic mystery of *Across the universe* or the acute particularity that makes songs like *Eleanor Rigby* such passionate if ironic moral statements, the tune and the sturdy triadic harmony justify the exhortation 'When the broken hearted people Living in the world agree, There will be an answer LET IT BE'.

In a sense the Gospel elements in this music relate it back to the communal music of the Beatles' first phase; and in *Let it Be* that songs that aren't hymnic are, though often surprising, unambiguously happy. Thus in *Two of us* the pals (not lovers, which is inevitably a more difficult relationship) ride together in A major parallel thirds, enlivened by a few cross accents, but making homewards without apprehension or regret. John's *Dig a pony*, though less homey, is no less delight-giving: a triple rhythmed boogie song of celebration, with ecstatic arabesques in eights against sixes. Several simple rock songs are rehashes of early material. *I've got a feeling* is a hard rock number riddled with blue notes and perhaps with a slight whiff of parody in its soul-singing; yet it's early Beatle music, the ebullience of which remains positive in effect. So does the barrelhouse style – again full of blue false relations but almost devoid of modulation – of *One after 909*, a rehash of a song John wrote when he was seventeen. Also in direct barrelhouse style is *Get back*, which in very high tessitura exhorts both man and girl to 'get back where you once belonged'. The words might seem to apply to the Beatles themselves: only of course we know, and the Beatles knew, that getting back to a Liverpudlian Eden was no longer possible. Though the dream was over, everything had been changed by it.

The chronology of *Let it Be* is obscure. Much of the material is, as we have seen, very early; even the new songs, such as *Across the universe* and *The long and winding road* were released as singles before *Abbey Road* was made. The LP of *Let it Be* seems to have been issued last mainly because the Beatles, totally disabused over their abortive film session on *Let it Be*, bickered over which songs were to be included, lost interest in the whole affair. John seems to regard the issue of the disc as intentionally suicidal: 'We didn't want to know about it any more, so we just left it to Glyn Jones and said Here, mix it. That was the first time since the first album that we didn't want to have anything to do with it . . . I had thought it would be good to let the shitty version out because it would break the Beatles, break the myth. It would be just us, with no trousers on and no glossy paint over the cover, and no hype: this is what we are like with our trousers off, would you please end the game now.' In fact it didn't turn out like that, because Phil Spector worked on the disc and made something of it, even on John's admission: 'he was given the shittiest load of badly recorded shit, with a lousy feeling toward it, ever. And he made something of it . . . When I heard it, I didn't puke.' Perhaps that was why the Beatles were able to end with the equivocal nobility of *The end*. Though most of the songs on *Let it Be* are good and entertaining and two or three of them are fine and touching, they are not and could not be exploratory. Like *Glass onion*, they're a wave over the shoulder and a goodbye, the happiness of which was deceptive. The title has its allegorical point; the disintegration of the Beatles 'corporate identity' was under way.

Part Four
Exit and
Lament

7. The Beatles Soli

We have seen that the Beatles' initiation was their discovery of their Liverpudlian corporate identity. As they grew up their Rubber Souls, armed with Revolvers, strayed into euphoric Penny Lane and hallucinatory Strawberry Fields; and attained a consummation which owes its power to the fact that their corporate identity allows for such complex nuances of personal stress and distress. Though Sgt. Pepper was pepperily militant in dragooning the circus band, the band itself played to a club of Lonely Hearts. That great record created a solidarity of the youthful whilst being at once pathetically and ironically aware of the solitariness of all hearts, young and old. The songs never proselytise, yet are genuinely a 'criticism of life'.

It was too much to expect that the delicate balance of *Sgt. Pepper* could be sustained. Yet the Beatles' third period, initiated on their *Magical Mystery Tour* and achieving fruition in *Abbey Road*, is a further stage in their evolution in that it accepts, unequivocally and unafraid, whatever darkness, as well as light, rebirth and regression may throw up. That is an astonishing achievement: especially if one thinks of the Beatles against the backcloth of the pop music industry in which they had been nurtured. Nor is it surprising that this precarious honesty was also impermanent. The beginning of disintegration was inherent in it; and although the Beatles threw retrospective glances back at their seemingly distant past (six years feels like a lifetime when you're young), they were then obliged, if not content, to Let it be, and to go their separate ways.

Before we can approach them as individualities, we should enquire rather more deeply into the nature of their corporate identity. I have commented, early on, on the general significance of the phenomenon of the 'group'; the case of the Beatles would seem to suggest that a group's success depends on the magnetic attractions and repulsions of its component members. There's an almost cosmological flavour about the Beatles' relationship to one another, with Paul and John, George and Ringo, as opposite poles. Ringo, smallish, squat, sturdy, is of the earth earthy, vocally broad Liverpudlian, instrumentally a drummer, beating his drums and through them the earth, measuring Time. As drummer, he's basic and sound rather than brilliant; he keeps things going, powerfully and affirmatively, but admits that when anything untoward or especially imaginative is required he 'does what the others tell me'. Indeed, his relative deficiency in flair emphasises both his dependence on and necessity to his colleagues. What Baby Dodds, greatest of early New Orleans jazz drummers, said of himself would apply to Ringo also: 'I work with them because they all belong to me. I feel I'm the keyman in that band. In drumming you have got to pay attention to each, everyone. You must *hear* that person distinctly, and hear what he wants. You got to give it to him. You must study a guy's human nature, study about what he will take, or see about what he will go for. All that's in a drum, and that's why all guys are not drummers that's drumming . . . Now I know it sounds very funny to hear me say spirit. *But drumming is spirit.* You got to have that in your body, in your soul . . . And it can't be an evil spirit . . . If you're evil, you're going to drum evil, and if you drum evil, you're going to put evil in somebody else's mind. What kind of a band have you got then? Nothing but an evil spirit band. And God help an evil spirit band. They're subject to anything. They're liable to step on each others instruments. Anything. Might put limburger cheese in a man's piano. Anything . . . So you got to keep a spirit up. And it's a drummer's job . . . His place is to help the other fellow, not play himself to death. Without a drummer that knows how to *help*, there's no band.' So Ringo's rock-bottom earthiness is a *giving*, and his measuring of the beat of Time in fact obliterates it. There is thus an inseparable tie-up between Ringo's thumping beat and the eternal drones favoured by George, his opposite. It isn't, after all, all that inappropriate that Ringo should wear magic talismantic rings, and that his second name should be STAR(R).

In the early years Ringo was simply there, whilst the other

Beatles rode on his beat, accepted his 'good spirit'. He was necessary, but subservient, to the brilliant composing duo Lennon and McCartney: whilst George, though clearly subservient, seemed more shadowy both in personality and in function. Ringo's function as drummer was obvious and important enough; George as instrumentalist was not thus basic, nor as singer – known to the other Beatles as 'the invisible singer' – did he often take the lead. Compensatorily, he occasionally composed songs; and through his songs his necessity to the foursome was gradually manifest. Without his increasing magnetic attraction the Beatles could not have grown from their original childish Eden to that interfusion of the corporeal and the spiritual, and of subconscious forces light *and* dark, which we have seen to characterise their mature creations. Even in the first years there are few Harrison numbers in strict rock style; his love songs tend to be romantic, even nostalgic, sublimating sexual desire into man's eternal and unappeasable longing for wholeness: so in a simple way he has always been a 'religious' composer, and his later addiction to quasi-Indian techniques and instruments – to drones, melismatic monody, microtonal variation, sitar and tabla – was a logical extension from first premises. If Ringo is a common bloke with a starry name, George Harrison is a guy with an everyday name and soulful yearnings, volatile Water to Ringo's Earth. His function, as Ringo's polar opposite, is still evident in the post-Beatles period. For although George's beautiful *While my guitar gently weeps* abandons his habitual orientalism in favour of magical folk-ritual collateral with the Lennon–McCartney Fool songs, George's number is still potently 'religious' in flavour, the winging pentatonic lines having an almost plainsong or troubadour-like fervour. His influence is surely felt too in the Gospel-style songs of *Let it Be*. Though he didn't compose them, they would seem to be prototypes for the Gospel songs in his solo album, when the religious impulse has become specifically and (the music suggests) genuinely Christian.

It's interesting that, almost immediately after the Beatles' break-up, Ringo – who had seldom sung, almost never composed, and whose function has been percussively basic – issued a solo

LP, *Sentimental Journey*, featuring himself not as drummer, but
as singer. It's as though he'd been wanting to break out, as well
as up; and the music he produces has little to do either with the
Beatles' innocent initiation or with their subtler consummation.
True, neither *Sentimental Journey* nor his later and better album
Beaucoups of Blues is Ringo's own music; he wishes he could
compose songs 'like the others', but admits that he can't. Still,
the songs he chooses – by composers called Pierce, Kingston,
Howard, about whom the sleeve proffers no information, not even
their Christian names – presumably reflect his tastes. Considering
their musical substance, which is for the most part routine, one
marvels afresh at Lennon–McCartney's inventive genius; but it
doesn't follow that because Ringo's *Beaucoups of Blues* is almost
totally insignificant as musical composition it is therefore without
character. Indeed, it's appropriate that Ringo should have produced a solo disc that relies on character more than musicianship, for his contribution to the group had always been his sterling
commonness, a gruffness and bluffness that yet made him lovable.
He once said: 'We're unassuming, unaffected and British to the
core. Someone once asked me why I wore rings on my fingers
and when I told him it was because I couldn't get them on my
nose he didn't believe me.' It's this typically British, throwaway
charm one finds on Ringo's solo disc: though superficially his
model is American country music, in particular Johnny Cash,
whose vocal quality as well as style Ringo sedulously imitates.
His tone is rounder, less blunt than it used to be; and even when
he sings of melancholic or melodramatic events, as in *Love doesn't
last long*, the music is easy, the manner bland, without the rasp,
let alone the apocryphal quality, of Dylan even in his later
country vein, when he too pays tribute to Johnny Cash. That
the songs can be escape songs in a way that the Lennon–McCartney
songs aren't is a consequence of the endearing simplicity of
Ringo's nature; but it's significant that the numbers work best
when escape in fact transports him home. The title song is about
coming Home because 'I've had enough'. The most fetching song
on the disc – *Draw* – is a letter to mum, in American country
guitar style, which manages to incorporate a reference to Bolton

city; whilst *Wine, women and loud happy songs* is an elegy on fame and fortune couched in terms of the old English music-hall or working men's club. Though the music offers nothing intrinsically beyond its models, Ringo's presentation of it acquires an element of comic pathos; only in the anti-war song *Silent homecoming* does the 'simplesse' seem to good to be true.

Ringo's need to break out would seem, however, to have been mild compared with George's: which, given their respective temperaments, is what one might expect. Scandal (who is often a lying jade) has it that accomplished Paul adopted a somewhat condescending attitude to George's musicianship. However this may be, George, in launching himself solo, stretched to no mere double, but to a triple, album; and employed a large number of highly professional assistants. Though the sophistication and even the sheer size of the resources are not an unqualified asset, they cannot merely be dismissed as a product of pique – of a desire to 'show us', and particularly to show Lennon and McCartney, what their once reticent colleague is capable of. For the resources are genuinely relevant to the nature of the music: which is technically more assured than any of George's songs before *While my guitar gently weeps*, and consistently tends towards fulfilment in the 'religious' terms we have seen to be characteristic of most of George's representative work.

In the early days George had composed, if exceptionally, a few hard-driving rock songs. In *All Things Must Pass*, his solo triple album, such songs appear again, in more expansive form. *Wah wah* and *What is life* are pulverising in rhythmic impetus, potent in blue melodic arabesque, audacious in harmonic assault (for instance, the sudden stab of A flat dominant seventh in the pounding F major of *Wah wah*, or, in *What is life*, the side-stepping between E flat, G flat and D flat). The instrumental parts are elaborate, highly exciting, and superbly played. The main difference between these songs and the comparable numbers from the early days is that they go on for a long time; and in so doing build up, incrementally, to communal ecstasy. Though they may start from the celebration of sexual energy (released in the pounding beat, the melodic breaks, the harmonic stabs), they end by obliterating Time far more radically than the early Beatle songs. Moreover, the sheer, unremittent continuity and enveloping reverberation of the sound becomes organistic no less than orgasmic: so we're not altogether surprised that the sexual rock songs merge imperceptibly into the specifically religious numbers which, having shed their orientalism, have become powerfully English transformations of Gospel shouts, complete with antiphonal alleluyas.

These swinging hymnic tunes have their prototype, we have seen, in *Let it Be*. The celebration of Christ or Krishna in *My sweet Lord*, *Awaiting on you all*, or *Hear me Lord* uses precisely the same technical means as the celebration of Woman in *What is life* – the enveloping sonority, the thrusting, syncopated beat, the shouted modal tune with prevailingly pentatonic riffs, the sudden harmonic lurch (for instance the diminished seventh after the pentatonics in *My sweet Lord*), the immense, slow build-up, with gradually increasing instrumental forces. This discredits neither Christ nor Woman, but rather stresses the authenticity of George's experience, whether or no we're willing to be engulfed by it. Yet there is both a paradox and a danger in such songs: which is that in being once more ritual they call for communal participation. As 'art', listened to on disc, they may seem inflated: whereas one of the supreme virtues of Beatle music has been its precise equilibrium between means and ends, with never a hint of self-indulgence. What is wrong with George's Gospel songs is what is wrong with the experience: which is not false, but simple-minded. In our complex modern society salvation cannot be won simply by an unremitting beat, a purely pentatonic doodle, and an engulfing sonority sustained for however long a time – which is about all, in musical substance, that *Hear me Lord* offers. Even when the tunes are genuinely catchy (and *catching* is what Gospel songs are supposed to be) one feels that they proffer answers without having asked the right questions. Significantly, the finest Harrison songs in *All Things Must Pass* are those which discover affinities between the religious and the personal-sexual levels of experience. They do ask questions – disturbing questions; and they give no easy answers.

I'd have you any time is especially interesting from this point of view, since it is a rehash of a number by Bob Dylan, who has perhaps influenced George as a composer more than the other composing Beatles. The re-creation comes out, however, as highly personal to George, in the lyrical-religious vein he established with *While my guitar gently weeps*. It begins in enveloping introversion – an effect achieved by alternating triads of tonic and flattened mediant, both with unresolved dissonant major sevenths and with an undulating pentatonic melody that painfully acquires blue false relations. The song is an appeal for union and communion in every sense; and as togetherness happens the vocal melismata gradually expand into plainsong or troubadour-like elation. The harmonic laceration of those dissonant sevenths and the instability of the Vaughan-Williams-style parallel triads are sustained throughout a continuous texture, with no 'middle'; yet the warm, close sonority nurses the pain – and lyrically liberates the tune. Even more remarkable is *Let it down*, which also opens with potently syncopated tonic triads with added sharp sevenths; hurtles, with anguished wonderment, to the flat submediant with added seventh on the phrase 'I can feel you here'; and cadences by way of a descending chromatic bass with weirdly enharmonic implications. Again there is no contrasting 'middle' but a cumulative refrain over a long tonic pedal with fierce passing dissonances and a pentatonic 'shout' as he asks her to 'let your hair hang all around me'. All the sexual connotations of hair are thus invoked in this disturbingly orgiastic song which – as we drown in her hair, the sea of sound and the waters of the unconscious – identifies the sexual and the religious impulse.

Another and still stranger descent beneath the waters occurs in *Beware of Darkness* which invites us to BE like a tree, aspiring upwards yet rooted to the earth, as an alternative to human distress. Darkness is magically evoked by a tonality that, unlike the tree, is rootless, oscillating between mediants and triads a tone apart. The weird twist from G major with flat seventh to a G sharp minor triad *enacts* the 'beware' of the verses, just as the shift from C sharp minor to D major to C creates the 'aimless' wandering of 'each unconscious sufferer'. The melody itself meanders – mostly pentatonically, but with a tritonal leap and a blue false relation on 'That's not what you're here for': which is the climax if the term is valid in reference to a song concerned with the opposite of progression. Both verse and music are mysterious and beautiful, and they work; we do *let go*, as the music ultimately declines in triads of B, A and G major, the last with a flat seventh, left unresolved.

I dig love is hardly less mysterious, though this time the equivocation is rhythmic rather than harmonic and tonal. A chromatic ostinato in parallel tenths, with persistent syncopation on the last quaver of the groups of four, oddly holds back impetus so that what would appear to be a simple celebration of love comes out as expectant, enquiring, wondering – waiting for a melodic revelation that in this song, despite the pentatonic riff-like refrain, does not happen. This gives point to the middle section, which contrasts the taking of love with the giving of it. Again, George is asking the questions to which there is no easy answer: as he is in *Run of the mill*, where ambiguity of choice is musically manifest in the curiously rocking cross rhythm and in a vacillation between D major and B minor, the cadences repeatedly contradicting expectation. There's a similar equivocation in *The Ballad of Sir Frankie Crisp*, a pseudo-medieval song built on a descending scale ostinato, which opens up strange horizons by way of mediant transitions. The words are about illusion and reality, love and light; and although the song is presented as a fairy-tale, its mythology is close to that of the religious-sexual songs on which we have commented. Even the charming 'country' songs usually retain a whiff of religious ecstasy (the tritonal syncopations in the refrain of *Apple scruffs*) or wonder (the disturbance of the open, triadic tune of *Behind the locked door* with the flat seventh harmonisation on the phrase 'Let me take them from you'). A few numbers – the title song *All things must pass* and *The art of dying* – are 'personal' religious songs halfway between the love songs and the Gospel shouts; *The art of dying* is especially interesting in that its stepwise moving, consistently offbeat lyricism recalls the orientalism of

George's earlier religious numbers, yet powerfully recreates it in his English-hymnic manner.

The key-song in the collection, *Isn't it a pity*, fuses the three song types favoured by George as soloist, for it is at once love-song, rock song, and hymn. The words explicitly relate sexual love to compassion, asking 'Isn't it a pity, isn't it a shame, how we break each other's hearts and cause each other pain'; and even the false rhyme underlines the song's bewildered honesty, with its musical punning on the sharp, upward aspiring feeling of the lydian fourths in the melody as contrasted with the harmonic thrust downwards on the natural fourths. Sometimes the sharpened fourths change enharmonically into flattened fifths, promoting one of those harmonic 'lurches' we've noticed in Harrison's rock songs. Yet the anguish within the music generates a slow exfoliation of lyricism; the once broken line grows gradually more sustained until it's fulfilled in instrumental ritornello, with winging vocal melismata. Metamorphosed into a hymn, the song has acquired some of the inflation we commented on in other hymnic pieces. None the less, the tune is very fine and we can understand why George repeats it as the penultimate song on side 2. The second version, being consummated, doesn't evolve, but sings for the most part over a tonic pedal.

These discs establish Harrison as a real composer, with an identity very different from Lennon and McCartney. He was younger than and subservient to what John has called, with no false modesty, their brilliance ('I couldn't be bothered with George when he first came around. He used to follow me around like a bloody kid, hanging around all the time . . . He was a kid who played guitar . . . It took me years to come around to him, to start considering him as an equal or anything.') He hasn't their priceless gift for the inevitably memorable tune, nor their wit, their unexpectedly mature recognition of 'other modes of experience that may be possible'; indeed his songs are almost never funny, though they are sometimes blithe. None the less, his feeling for a runic, magical poetry and his exploration of harmonic and tonal mysteries are both personal and poignant; and it would seem that, in his quieter way, he knows what he

wants and has in him to do. It's worth noting that George's
score for Joe Massot's film *Wonderwall* (composed for a dis-
tinguished band of mostly Indian musicians) is at once aurally
imaginative and cinematically effective: though it perhaps
shouldn't have been issued as an LP since it hasn't the sustained
musical interest which, in the context of the film, it didn't need
and might even have been the worse for.

As a performer George's talents parallel his composing ability.
His guitar playing has always been sensitive. In the early days it
was he who maintained a musically dedicated attitude, insisting
on the correct tuning of their instruments even when they were
inaudible because of girlish screams; on the new solo album – in
so far as it is possible to assess his contribution – he seems to
stand up as guitarist to the august company he keeps. As for
his voice, if it lacks Paul's plangency, John's wide emotional
range, or even Ringo's bearish charm, it is beautifully apposite,
in its very attenuation, to his most representative songs. I do not
know whether George himself or producer Phil Spector was
responsible for the elaborate resources employed in *All Things
Must Pass*; since his finest numbers are the most intimate, I hope
he may have the courage to produce an album less reliant on
adventitious support, excellent though its quality may be.

If Ringo and George are polar opposites who needed one
another, the same is true of the more significant because creative
duo of John and Paul. Their relationship, as one might expect, is
more complex; and though one cannot merely describe them as
Fool and Walrus, with Paul as the positive, John as the negative,
pole, such a distinction will serve as starting point. John is the
mixed up iconoclast, the doubter, prone to deflationary irony,
addicted to the verbal pun. Whilst his published 'ritings' hardly
pretend to be more than a post-Joycean game, his obsession with
verbal ambiguity is pertinent to his poetic and musical gifts;
significantly, he thinks *Across the universe* is one of his best
songs because 'it's good poetry, or whatever you call it, without
chewing it. See, the ones I like are the ones that stand out as
words, without melody'. Paul, on the other hand, is more impressive in purely, or perhaps one should say conventionally, musical

skills. His art is lyrical and extrovert, relatively uncontorted even when fierce, and he's prone to non-personal narrative and balladic songs. John's art is introvert and more intense, his verses frequently being concerned with personal experience. After the first few years Lennon and McCartney didn't often compose together, and it would seem to be broadly true that they take the lead in their own compositions. None the less, Paul's Air needed John's Fire, just as Ringo's Earth needed George's Water. Opposite poles generate electricity. Between John and Paul the sparks flew; John's fiery iconoclasm was tempered by Paul's airy grace, whilst Paul's wide-eyed charm was toughened by John's resilience. Perhaps it isn't entirely fortuitous that, especially on the evidence of their solo albums, John shows a partiality for sharp keys such as A, F sharp minor and E major, Paul for flat keys such as B flat, E flat and A flat. However this may be, some of Paul's finest songs are sharply satirical without surrendering their lyricism: whereas John's finest songs discover a lyricism that is both mysterious and disturbing. This means that, solo, John and Paul are, as composers, put to a stern test: it does not follow that they will be unequal to it. Their future fascinates, for the new, post-1950 pop is an art-ritual of adolescence, and we have yet to discover what happens when youth is spent. Corporately, the Beatles matured astonishingly and unpredictably within a brief seven years. It remains to be seen whether, each alone, John and Paul can survive; and if so whether they must become a radically different type of artist.

Paul's musical skills are impressively evident on his first solo LP, simply called *McCartney*, and perhaps it's significant – with reference to the Beatles' earlier history – that the album's verbal interest is minimal. Many of the songs, indeed, are Edenic, like the earliest Beatle songs: except that their musical sophistication enables us to respond to them as having 'been through' the Beatle experience. If Paul hasn't noticeably been scared *by* it, he's preserved his innocence *through* it, so that the music comes out fresh as a new pin. Mal Evans has neatly characterised McCartney the composer as 'champion of the softedge, a knight errant rescuing discarded sentiments, rehabilitating sensibilities that time has hardened into clichés . . . The components of Paul's songs are lovingly assembled like the parts in a vintage car. All the machinery is polished (it's a clean machine). Their excellence is how they are put together; all the pieces fit beautifully. Crazy, lazy, frantic, Atlantic; words evoking a whole era. Bottled 20's essence; Astaire, talkies, the Black Bottom, Mickey Mouse is born, Rocky Raccoon, Eleanor Rigby, Maxwell's Silver Hammer, Honey Pie, Joe-Joe, the fireman with an hour-glass, Sgt. Pepper, Desmond and Molly Jones live in this magic landscape . . . in which all holidays, weddings, honeymoons and good times take place. Brief festivals of love set in the drab day-to-day world. Penny Lane has its opposite in the 'real' world: 1967 was the year of the "month of Sundays", an attempt to regain the golden age under the banner of Sgt. Pepper.' In his first solo album McCartney seems to have made this Arcadia, this 'mirror image of the real world, where birds sing, and lyrics grow on trees', come true: for most of the songs are love songs, addressed to his Linda, whom he seems securely to have married, after his relatively randy youth; or to the kids in his country retreat. The first song on the album is indeed basic, consisting simply of a happy, child-like chanting of a pentatonic phrase on the words, '*Lovely Linda*, with the lovely flowers in her hair'. The cantillation dances and prances across the beat; the ostinato pattern of the guitar repeats, unchanging, a simple blues progression in Country-Western style. *That would be something* is similar, but subtler. The 'talismantic' phrase is here: 'It really would be something to meet you in the falling rain'. The hesitant expectancy (with an undercurrent of fear) is conveyed through the syncopated and contracted rhythm for 'would be something', whilst the falling rain phrase is a pentatonic doodle which sometimes turns into wordless humming or vocalising, often in falsetto (see Ex. 62). The harmony consists exclusively of dominant sevenths, subdominants and tonics in oscillation; and the song generates a subdued wonder from continual slight variations on the verbal phrase, the melodic pattern, the metrical stresses, and the techniques of vocal production.

Oo you is another love-spell addressed to Linda. The guitar

Ex. 62

That would be some - thing___ To meet you in the fal - ling rain.

___ Mom-ma meet you in the fal - ling rain___

Oo hm hm___

part is elaborate and superbly played, its conventions being those of black, country blues guitar, with flat sevenths, clanking acciaccaturas, portamento sobs and sighs. Yet the total effect is again child-like rather than wild: partly because the metre is so sharply defined and the playing so polished, partly because the voice's pentatonic roulades, often in falsetto, are exuberantly comic. This in no way discredits the happiness nor the authenticity of the piece as a love song. Another and much wilder blues song

is *Maybe I'm amazed*, which has an introduction in D major-
minor, but a verse which contradicts the key signature by
vacillating between triads of B flat and C, with occasional sidesteps
to F and G, and a climax created by the bass's chromatic descent
to an A flat triad with added sixth. The chorus, or middle, is in D,
but pierced with blue false relations of major and minor third,
often sounded simultaneously. The vocal line is very high throughout, yelling in soul style, and straining to a high F natural when
he tells us that she's the only woman who could ever help him.

Ex. 63

The final yodelling melisma is ecstatic; and indeed the whole
song manages to be 'amazed' in its wild blueness, yet unambiguously joyful. Despite the Negroid influence, this blueness
isn't black.

Sometimes the 'soul' song shades into Anglo-American ballad.
Every night, with a regular pulsing accompaniment in quavers,
has a folk-hymnic quality, suggesting early American country
music in its overlapping of dominants with their tonic resolution.
The tune moves gently, by step or in thirds or fourths; the

oo-oo-ooing refrain is technically speaking a rhythmic break – which literally effects a break in Time. *Man, we was lonely* is not so much a ballad as a raggy music-hall song with oompah bass. Here the tune, in parallel thirds to epitomise togetherness, is consistently diatonic, rocking between third and fourth; but the middle (telling us how he used to ride alone before he found HOME) is jazzily syncopated and tonally restless, swaying between B flat with flat seventh and F minor. *Teddy boy*, one of the few songs that has no connection with love and Linda, is also a music-hall number, and one of some subtlety. It's a narrative ballad telling of a boy called Ted who can't adjust to his mum's second marriage or liaison. The square rhythm and simple tonics and dominants of the opening are contradicted by the comic-pathetic, broken 'pentatonic' thirds on 'Ted be good, he would'.

The middle, with abrupt shifts to the mediant G, and then to C major, suggests Ted's perturbation, and even involves us in it. Yet this is a typical McCartney song in that it is at once tender and amused; and one might say the same of the most beautiful

and characteristic song in the album, *Junk*. This describes a
junk shop in a lyrical McCartney waltz tune, with a dotted
rhythm swing. The elided syncopation at the end of the vocal
phrase (on the words 'jubilee and 'for') gives to the nostalgia a
wistfulness remote from sentimentality; and it's interesting that
the 'middle', in B flat major introduced with the *minor* of the
subdominant with flattened seventh, is more resonantly emotive
than the lilting G minor verse. This fits the words, for whereas
the verse merely describes the junk, the middle asks a question:
'Buy, buy says the sign in the shop window, Why, why says the
junk in the yard?' The haunting little tune – especially the
falsetto vocalise in the coda –

Ex. 65

makes inanimate objects become the fragmented dreams of youth:
as is still more touchingly manifest when, on side 2, the piece is
repeated in purely instrumental form, the guitar sighful, plangent
almost to the point of heartbreak. Paul's instrumental virtuosity
is here inseparable from his composing talent, as it is in the fast
instrumental numbers such as *Valentine's Day* (with high, 'crying'
chromatics on guitar) and *Hot as sun* (with complex rhythmic
contrarieties.) Electronic effects of double tracking, etc., are also
as imaginative as they are unpretentious, enhancing, and sometimes literally echoing, the fine guitar playing.

   John Lennon's first solo LP, *Plastic Ono Band*, complements
McCartney in being its polar opposite. It too deals with personal
love as against corporate activity: only whereas *McCartney's*
verbally minimal approach makes for a happy, sophisticatedly

innocent music, Lennon's 'underground' songs start from words, which stimulate a music both primitive and deeply melancholy. Yet Lennon has his own kind of sophistication, for the sequence of songs is planned, no less than *Sgt. Pepper*, as a whole. We begin with *Mother* which, after a tolling of funeral bells, cuts the ties of family, saying goodbye in successive stanzas to mother, father and children, in a rigidly frozen metre so slow that it seems liable at any moment to cease. The vocal line consists of primitive 'tumbling strains', with pentatonic arabesques and blue flattened sevenths like a Gospel shout; and it too is fragmented, threatened with complete stasis. The variety of nuance and inflection on the Goodbyes, though Lennonesque and English, is worthy of the finest Negro soul singer. The sense of imminent breakdown leads

Ex. 66

to a coda that scarily reverses the verbal meaning of the stanzas; with a change in rhythm John lurches into a desperate ululation MAMA DON'T GO DADDY COME HOME: which rises to a scream, then fades out as they take no notice.

Left alone, he tells us, or rather tells himself, to *Hold on*; and
if he does 'it's gonna be all right' and (with Yoko's help) 'we're
gonna win the fight'. But the beat – still handled by Ringo,
incidentally – is nervously jittery, with recurrent silences; and the
tune, though lyrical, is still a pentatonic tumbling strain, fragmented, breaking the sense of the sentences, so that we hang
precariously in the middle of the 'gonna be all right' phrase,
wondering if we'll ever land. The melismata on 'hold on' and
'make the flight' are tender, but tentative:

Ex. 67

So the positive qualities of this most moving song are exploratory
rather than assured; John has described it beautifully in comment-
ing that it's 'all right now, this moment, so hold on now; we
might have a cup of tea or we might get a moment's happiness
any minute now, so that's what it's all about, just moment by
moment; that's how we're living, cherishing each day and dreading
it too. It might be your last day – you might get run over by a

car – and I'm really beginning to cherish it.' The music – not merely these words – discovers a new and deeper meaning in the 'vulnerability' we commented on in early Beatle songs. Because the pain in these stretched and broken phrases hurts so much, the lyricism is that much more assuaging.

Tenderness is, however, brusquely brushed aside by the next song, *I found out*: which *is* assured, but only in denunciation. If *Mother* had exploded family ties, this song blows up the brother-friend relationship, for he's seen through junkies, Jesus, Hare Krishna, and has 'found out' what was indeed evident in the previous song – that 'it can't do you no harm to feel your own pain'. Musically, the piece is very primitive, pre-harmonic, in an almost consistently pentatonic unisonal chant, with one savagely tritonal chromatic for the 'I found out' refrain:

Ex. 68

Though there is no harmony, the rhythm is both irregular (with bars of 3/8 and 5/8 intruding into the basic 4/4) and disrupted by silences. The beat is fierce. *Working class hero* is also musically rudimentary, a Bob Dylan-style 'talking blues' Anglicised into a slow 9 or 6/8 lilt, with a droning accompaniment oscillating between the triads of A minor and G major with flat seventh. The only other chord is a D major triad in the chorus; this serves as dorian Amen in the coda. The talking vocal line is launched, as it were, by an upward leaping sixth E to C: from which point it droops of its own weight, by step or by pentatonic minor thirds. John says it's a revolutionary song, but its spirit is stoic rather than militant, as it differentiates Them (who 'hurt you at home and hit you at school . . . kept you doped with religion and sex and TV . . . till you think you're so clever and classless and free') and Us, the young, whose isolation is complete.

And *Isolation* is indeed the title of the last song on side 1: which is an (again Anglicised) version of Negro piano blues, beginning with an ostinato that recalls the great Jimmy Yancey. The piano's bare, open fifths suggest the emptiness of isolation ('we're afraid to be alone'); the scrunchy chromatic passing dissonances (moving from A to A sharp to B to C natural and down again, through the D major triad) convey an intensity of pain, timeless in the silent night. The bluesy tune is infinitely sad, its pentatonic phrases once more broken, lyrically undulating in thirds and sixths, yet incomplete, separated by silences, the melismata aspiring, but stifled:

Ex. 69

The 'middle', telling us we're 'just human, a victim of the insane', becomes rhythmically more agitated, with soul-style vocal yells; and the habitual false relations between F sharp and F natural are intensified because the F naturals are now harmonised not with the tonic D major triad, but with the dominant seventh of C.

The final stanza, however, sees our fear against the world's impermanence and the sun's eternity, re-establishing the music's blue gravity which, whatever the words say, withstands terror. In this powerful song Lennon has done something which the Beatles in their togetherness couldn't have done. He has created an English 1970 equivalent for the Negro blues, which is an urban folk art of the solitary heart. In this his achievement as an Englishman is collateral with Dylan's as a white American.

The second side of the disc precisely mirrors, but also intensifies, the first side. *Remember* again debunks childhood and youth: mum's and dad's dreams for you were no less phoney than the legends of TV and silver screen. Here the music is as minimal as are McCartney's words in *Lovely Linda*, for the vocal line is no line at all, but a series of pentatonic fragments splutteringly ejaculated. The tonality too is very odd, jerking between triads of C and A major (that may be a dominant of D minor), only to hammer on an E minor triad – which by way of a chromatically descending bass returns to C. So both melodically and tonally we're lost; and are conscious mainly of the remorselessly stabbing, nagging, loud, rapid, beat: which ends, however, by knocking us unconscious and literally blowing the past up – on Guy Fawkes night! An old-fashioned piano ballad imperceptibly steals on us, from far off. When the vocal line begins to sing of *Love* it's for real, as the tenderly floating melody – in a modal F sharp minor that is always seeking the security of D major – suggests. The words 'feeling' and 'reaching' are enacted by a tension between flat seventh in the instrumental part, sharp seventh in the vocal line; and on the word 'you' a declining melisma swings us wildly and wonderingly from a D major to an F major triad which then immediately rocks back to G (see Ex. 70). So once more the line is broken, and the ballad fades away on the old-world Alberti basses of the parlour piano, an intimation of immortality, yet too dreamy to survive the world we're born into. John thinks the tune is 'very beautiful', and he's right. What is still more remarkable about it is its innocence, after so many, so harried years.

The innocent dream which is also true ('we might get a minute's happiness, any moment now') is anyway dismissed by the next

Ex. 70

Love is you, _____ you and me,

song, ironically titled *Well, well, well*, a sinister beat number
obliterating all pentatonic Edens. Linearly, it's itself pentatonic,
though in a mode – based on F sharp rather than A – that incorporates the devilishly flattened tritonal fifth (F sharp to C natural)
rather than the godly perfect fifth. The stanzas are monophonic,

Ex. 71

Well Well Well,   oh __ well, __   Well Well

Well,   oh __ well. __

the savagely 'African' vocal being doubled by raucous fuzzbuzz
instrumentals, barely harmonised, with aggressively thumping
beat. The 'well, well, well' refrain has triadic harmony, but in
African antiphonal style, with no implied progression. The words
concern a failed love-relationship, set in the immediate present,

not in a childish or adolescent past. He takes his love out to dinner ('She looked so beautiful I could eat her'); they talk of revolution and Women's Lib; they go into a big field to 'watch the English sky'. Yet 'we were both nervous feeling guilty, and neither one of us knew just why'. So that cannibalistic impulse gains ascendancy; the primitive beat and the monophonic yells build up cumulatively, though with no modulation, only a frenetically obsessive oscillation between F sharp and A as bass. Finally the music becomes a voodooistic nightmare, the Well, well, well's a series of screams. Grown up John capitulates to the infant's hysteria, traumatically howling for the maternal breast. This may be almost literally true, for the song was written whilst John was undergoing Primal Therapy with Dr. Janov.

Left alone, he begins again, turning inward, enquiring Who am I? what am I supposed to be? This invitation to *Look at me* is gentle, with thinly spaced, nervously syncopated guitar and with a tune that might be a folk song if ever it got going. But it revolves round and round on itself, failing to sing, sometimes petering into silence. Similarly, the harmonic bass teeters between A and F sharp again, and its attempted modulation sharpwards fails. The refrain 'Oh my love, Oh my love' is a bemused appeal: which might possibly offer some kind of release, since in the last stanza the question 'Who am I?' is modified to 'Nobody else can see me, Just you and me, Who are we? Oh my love, Oh my love.' But the exclamations on 'Oh' make sighful G sharp appoggiaturas to the bass's F sharp, the resolution on to 'love' being wearily delayed (see Ex. 72).

So the hope, if that's what it is, would seem to be frail: as is manifest in the next and climacteric song *God* which, in both length and emotional weight, balances the *Isolation* song on side 1. *God* is a song of almost total rejection: for having told us in soul-style monodic plaint that 'God is a concept by which we measure our pain', the central section of the number consists of a catalogue of 'don't believes' in quasi-monodic incantation with intensifying percussion. The list covers I Ching, the Bible, Tarot, Hitler, Jesus, Kennedy, Buddha, Yoga, Kings, etc., ending with 'I don't believe in Beatles': followed by a brief, intently silent

Ex. 72

silence; and then unaccompanied, in lyrical pentatonicism, 'I
believe in me, Yoko and me'; and then, spoken, 'And that's
reality'. The final section of the song is again lyrical and basically
pentatonic, but with a minatory percussive ostinato. It tells us
that 'the dream is over' and dismisses Beatle mythology: 'I was
the dreamweaver . . . I was the walrus, But now I'm John.' The
tiny epilogue, however, prevents our taking this self-reliance with
easy optimism: for *My mummy's dead* may express the release he
asked for in the first song of the cycle, yet does so in a sickening
cross between nursery rhyme (it opens with the descending scale
of Three Blind Mice) and TV commercial jingle. If it takes us
back to the childhood the Beatles had started from, it's utterly
disabused and disillusioned. 'It's hard to explain So much pain,
I never could show it, My Mummy's dead.'

The powerful effect of these Lennon solo songs is even more
than normally misrepresented by any attempt at written notation:
this is 'oral' music that can be realised only by way of oral techniques. None the less, on the evidence of these first two solo LPs

of McCartney and Lennon, it would seem that, whereas Paul's innocently sophisticated musicianship wouldn't be likely to develop without qualities analogous to John's experience, John's experience could and would acquire the kind of musicianship it needed. This seems to be borne out by their second solo discs: for whereas Paul's *Ram* is a pleasant record that adds nothing to *McCartney*, John's *Imagine* is a more positive development from songs such as *Isolation*. In *Ram* there are relatively few straight love songs, though *Long haired lady* is the most original song in the album, achieving a typical fusion of comedy and awe by way of equivocations between a pentatonic E minor in the tune and sophisticated sidesteps between G major-minor, C major-minor and E flat major in the instrumentals:

Ex. 73

Most of the numbers are country songs. *Too many people*, Paul tells us, are 'pulled and pushed around': so he and Linda and the kids seek love in country solitude and a stepwise moving tune with a lovely refrain – safeguarded from mooniness by a precarious ambiguity between tonic, subdominant and subdominant of the subdominant (so that the tune starts off on the triad of the flat seventh). Similarly *Back seat of my car* seeks happiness in simple togetherness ('we believe we can't be wrong'), creating a love song of the vowels dreamily melismatic, flexible in rhythm: while *Heart of the country* has a catchy tune in Country-Western boogie style, pentatonic, but with blue false relations and sophisticatedly chromatic harmonies. *Ram on* is a rideaway song, with an expansive modal tune somewhat frustrated by a complex nagging beat; *Three legs* employs ingenious syncopation to emulate a dog's three-legged lollop; and *Uncle Albert* is parodistically rejected with a lyricism almost benign. While it wouldn't be fair to call these numbers escape songs, since Paul and Linda and the kids have made this dream come true, it would perhaps be valid to say that both the lyricism and the wit come a little easily. One is grateful to join, even vicariously, in a happiness that, the music suggests, is genuine, and one appreciates vocal and instrumental performance that is precisely articulated, as sensitive as it is agile. Even so, it is difficult to see where Paul, with Linda and without John, can go from here. In the past his finest achievements – with the possible exception of ostensibly nostalgic songs like *Yesterday* – were in part released by John's awareness of 'the pain of consciousness'. It's precisely because John's second LP *Imagine is* concerned with the pain of consciousness that it can effect a positive growth from his previous disc, even though it is musically less sophisticated than Paul's solo performances.

The title song takes up, from the earlier record, the theme of rejection, asking us to imagine that there's no heaven, no hell, no possessions; then it transforms the theme into a positive vision of peace and the brotherhood of man. If this sounds pretentious – as the *words* of the first solo album often sound self-indulgent – the music makes the vision incarnate: for from an introverted, brooding texture of rocking arpeggios, all tonics and subdominants, a folklike (once more basically pentatonic) melody flowers. The melismata on 'some day' and 'join us' suggest potentiality, waiting to be fulfilled; strings halo the voice with modal gravity, and with no hint of cinematic gloss (see Ex. 74):

Ex. 74

I hope some day___ you'll join us___

From this vision *in potentia* we descend with a bump to
1920ish barrelhouse rag. *Crippled inside* uses the inane eupepticism
of this style to contrast the masks we wear in public with our
crippled inner selves; and for this effects a direct musical synonym,
since the 'mask' of the resolutely and cornily diatonic harmony
hides a tune that – except for one chromatic passing note – is
again consistently pentatonic. Through the collusion of words
with the music we recognise that our disguises are comparable with
those of the Black Faced Minstrel, and that we employ them for
similar ends. The farce of the conventionally rhetorical coda in
'half-time' (arms outstretched, toothy grin wider than ever) is
slightly horrid as well as funny; and lest we might think that he's
referring only to the other guy as 'crippled inside', John immediately follows this with a song of personal insecurity. Thematically,
Jealous guy sometimes recalls *A day in the life*, the almost-
mythic song of a generation; but it's also related to the 'lost'
songs on *Plastic Ono Band*. Its musical materials are again
rudimentary: a simple, pentatonic phrase, in echoing repetition,
a mere rising scale in cross rhythm to convey loss of control and a
'shivering inside' (see Ex. 75). Yet again the permutations of
rhythm and of vocal inflexion suggested by the words, and the
unexpected mediant triads that make us 'cry', are oddly positive in
effect, building up to an almost jaunty whistling refrain and to a
line that – in comparison with the fragmental utterances of *Plastic
Ono Band* – is lyrically sustained. Similarly, though *It's so
hard* is saying precisely that – living and loving are both difficult
and painful – the primitive, barrelhouse piano style is potent, the
ostinato compulsive, the Gospel-soul vocal line riddled with

Ex. 75

false relations and sharp lydian fourths, doubled with fuzzbuzz, so that the sonority has a harsh, rock-bottom reality comparable with that of the genuine primitive blues:

Ex. 76

One can understand why John has come to love the blues no less than, even more than, his rudimentary rock: considering when and where the blues derived from, it can only be that much more 'real'.

Here the potential we detected in *Isolation*, on the previous disc, is being fulfilled; as it is in a rather different sense in the big song that concludes side 1. Superficially, this again looks like a song of rejection: *I don't wanna be a soldier* (sailor, failure, rich man, poor man, beggar man, thief, churchman, etc.): these rejections being chanted, like those in *God*, to an even-rhythmed undulation, a tone up and a tone down around a nodal point. But this time the monodic incantation, primitively liturgical in flavour, is sustained, and gradually intensified, against a remorseless pentatonic ostinato, whilst non-harmonic instrumental figurations build up a furious hubbub resembling a voodoo ceremony at full tilt. The 'world' outside us indeed seems to be demonically possessed; and finally expires in electrophonic tweets and judders. Yet the vocal chant survives, indeed grows stronger: so that the ultimate rejection of its 'oh no no' refrain (in African homophony on the major third) becomes paradoxically a triumph (see Ex. 77).

The extraordinarily powerful effect of this song is directly relatable – as is that of some songs on Lennon's earlier solo LP – to what I've referred to as its voodooistic tendencies. For Haitian voodoo is a ritual neither secular nor Christian, but concerned with the interaction of the world of spirits and the world of men, between which (as Malcolm Bruce Corrie has put it) communication is impossible because of an original disharmony. 'However, men can recover the harmony if they know how to manipulate the forces which govern the world of nature. Rhythm provides the semantic bridge between the categories of the physical universe and the categories which define the bodily constitution of man. Merriam touched upon the general problem: "The production of physical response seems clearly to be an important function of music; the question of whether this is primarily a biological response is probably overridden by the fact it is culturally shaped . . ." The act of mediation is in fact an act of transformation. Both the rhythms which induce it and the trance condition itself are formally delimited and faithfully enacted, and all the symbols, including sound, express this fundamental

Ex. 77

act as surely as they produce it. It is, in the last analysis, an act of the mind.' This passage bears directly on the impact of Lennon's incantation, which is concerned precisely with bridging the gulf between the world of spirits and the material world of rich man, poor man, beggar man, thief. And its point lies in the fact that it is an act of possession that is also an 'act of the mind'. It exists on a disc; we may experience it, if we wish, in solitude – and at the same time in the presence of ghosts innumerable.

The first two songs on the second side repeat but modify the previous pattern. *Gimme some truth* is again a hard-driving rock song of rejection, denouncing 'uptight-short-sighted-narrow-minded hypocrites' with a wit comparable with Dylan's; again, hard physical energy and nagging repeated notes become life-enhancing. There is a particularly fine solo from George, whose presence on *Imagine* is a major reason for its superiority to *Plastic Ono Band*. *Oh my love* takes up the theme of the two-way love relationship against Society. Parlour piano substitutes for barrel-house piano, for the song is balladic, with no jazz or blues elements. Its corniness, however, is superficial; the tonality veers oddly between D major with lydian fourths and A major (with hints of B minor and F sharp minor), and the melismata on the phrases 'my eyes can see' and 'for the first time in my life', enact the new birth, hopefully, doubtfully, in our ears and heart.

Ex. 78

What is here tentative is consummated in *How do you sleep*, which on the surface seems a vicious anti-Paul song, beginning, indeed, with a quotation from McCartney's *You never give me your money!*

Apparently Sgt. Pepper took Paul by surprise; he lives with straights, jumps when his momma speaks to him; and makes a sound which is no more than muzak to John's ears. Yet whatever the personal malice and malignity, the music redeems it, and gives to the words a generalised application. Pepper took us *all* by surprise; and the question 'how do you sleep at night?' is pertinent to us all. In this sense the song contrasts the masks we present to the world – which other songs on the disc have torn asunder – with the reality within the subconscious, and in sleep. This may be why the tune, beginning with those assertive repeated notes, and a 'blue' arabesque to the flattened fifth, expands into pentatonic roulades:

Ex. 79

Those freaks was right when they said you was dead
The on-ly thing you done was yes-ter-day
The sound you make is Mu-zak to my ears

The song acquires a grave nobility, almost an heroic quality, worthy of comparison with the finest songs of Dylan in this vein. As an account of Paul's music, it's vitiated by rancour; as a statement about the human condition it's highly impressive – and an experience that, to be fair, we must suspect to be beyond Paul's range.

Characteristically, this sustained affirmation is followed immediately by another song of self-doubt. '*How* can I go forward when I don't know which way I'm facing, How can I feel something if I don't know how to feel.' Again the entirely diatonic song is basic in its musical material: a simple descending scale which unexpectedly stops; is punctured with thumping cadential chords; tries again, petering out in a chromatically wavering melisma; but ends in an *Oh no no* refrain that is also truncated, with instrumental cadences separated by briefly pregnant silences.

Ex. 80

Paradoxically again, the firmly diatonic and cadential nature of these broken phrases makes them quite different in effect from the stumbling fragmentation of the comparable songs on *Plastic Ono Band*. Indeed, they make an affirmation out of their however hesitant honesty; and strings derive from these chordal energies a soaring lyricism. This being so, the song can run into the final number, an unambiguous paean of love for Yoko. The rhythmic pulse is continuous, with a talismantic refrain that, however simple, doesn't need to be self-defensively ironic; and although the song is not intrinsically among the more interesting, its effect, in the context of the whole disc, is powerful. Its happiness seems at once tipsy, and therefore dangerous, in its rumba rhythms and also, in its sturdy dominant cadences, true. Its tonality, D flat, is for John unusual; perhaps one should regard it as enharmonically identical with C sharp major and consider the song as a 'major' complement to John's earlier and wonderful love song to Yoko,

Because: which is exploratorily in C sharp minor, key of the Moonlight Sonata.* In any case the revelation of *Because* is not superseded by the happiness of *O Yoko*: for we know that although *O Yoko* finally takes off into a Dylan-like, electronically distorted whining of harmonica, this Eden has been painfully won through to; and will need to be won through to again and again. The greatest tribute to this disc as a whole is that it grows, in its rudimentariness, increasingly impressive with familiarity: to have created a British equivalent for the Negro blues and for a voodoo ritual is no mean accomplishment.

A note on John and Yoko

Yoko Ono comes only peripherally into this book, which is a retrospect on the Beatles' achievement. Her appearance in John's life, indeed, coincides with the Beatles' mutual disintegration as a performing entity since, according to John, it was the other Beatles' alignment against her that drove the final nail into the Beatles' composite coffin. The clash of personalities, whatever it may have been, is of biographical, not musical, interest; none the less Yoko as representative of the avant-garde art-world is of relevance, for she has clearly influenced John's recent work deeply, as he has influenced her. Superficially it might seem that they are polar opposites, John a product of showbiz and commerce, Yoko of sophisticated chic. Yet Yoko's brand of visual, and to a lesser degree literary and musical, avant-garderie has latent affinities with the pop ethos; whatever one's estimate of her talents, they're clearly compatible with those of Andy Warhol in film, Roy Lichtenstein in painting, John Cage and Ornette Coleman, LaMonte Young and Terry Riley in music – and all these men create by rejecting the paraphernalia of 'Western' art. John's two solo LPs are in a sense the most primitive, the least 'arty' music he has created; they are also the deepest and

* *O Yoko* can also be seen as a positive counterpart to the negative *My mummy's dead* which ended *Plastic Ono Band*: this was also in C sharp minor, and in addition both songs share the *Three blind mice/All you need is love* refrain which is so fundamental to John's music.

truest; and it seems that Yoko helped him to discover his 'basic' self without trying to change it. As an oriental, she sometimes wondered why John's music had to be so rigorously obsessed with metrical Time. On the solo LPs the obsession is not released; but the elemental simplicity of the music comes out as *basic* as Yoko's cinematic confrontation of bare bums. John's comments on the avant-garde scene and what it's meant to him are honest but confused. His recent music is honest and unconfused; and it's never been more potently aware of its roots, untrammelled by the corruptions of showbiz or the pretentions of Art.

Nor is Yoko's own musical contribution negligible. When she first blossomed as singer-piper-crier-moaner it was in immediately pre-Lennon days, in collaboration with Ornette Coleman who has claims to be considered the deepest, most exciting jazz horn player now active. His sax is 'elemental' in being simultaneously human, bird-like, beast-like, insect-like: singing, speaking, chirping, chittering, grunting, groaning, sighing. Later, some of the Ono–Coleman music was put on the first of the Plastic Ono Band discs, Yoko providing the vocals with a group consisting of John on guitar, Ringo on drums and Klaus Voorman on bass, in consort with Ornette Coleman (playing trumpet, not sax) and his two brilliant bassists David Izenzon and Charles Haden, and his normal drummer Edward Blackwell. All the pieces are Yoko's, though the composition doesn't amount to much beyond the creation of a riff or ostinato to serve as support to improvisation by herself and Ornette, either solo or in dialogue. The disc is not altogether a success, partly because Coleman's superb jazz potential seems damped by the pinched, nasal orientalism of Yoko's squawks and squeeks, gibbers and judders; and partly because total freedom of vocal resource proves paradoxically a limitation, for having exhausted her repertory of noises Yoko repeats them – with decreasing impact. None the less, the disc contains magical moments, especially in the close, heterophonic exchanges between voice and trumpet; and the voodooistic hubbub at the end may well have provided impetus for the voodoo nightmares in *Well, well, well* and *I don't wanna be a soldier.*

John played on this first Plastic Ono Band record, but the creative work was Yoko's and Ornette's. John and Yoko first made music together on the curious disc called *Two Virgins*. This appeared in 1968, soon after the Yoko–Coleman collaboration (though the disc of the latter wasn't released until 1970). It was apparently an off-the-cuff improvised session, made in the small hours of the night; and is a failure because although Yoko 'does her thing' effectively enough, John has no chance to do *his* thing, and there is no Ornette Coleman and collaborators to provide backbone and sinew. The disc comes out as slack and self-indulgent; though occasionally the doodling sparks off, especially at the opening of side 2, which sounds like a bit of Harry Partch, that redoubtable grand old man of music-theatre's avant-garde.

Collaboration between John and Yoko really begins to work when he, under her sway, creates his *own* kind of music. In the year or so before the solo albums John produced some powerful rehashes of early numbers associated with, though not by, the juvenile Beatles – such as *Money* and *Dizzy Miss Lizzy*; and an impressive new version of his *Abbey Road* favourite, *Yer Blues*. He also wrote a number of new songs – *The Ballad of John and Yoko*, *Instant Karma*, *Cold turkey*, *Power to the People* – that anticipate in their rocky starkness and immediacy the consummation to be achieved on the solo albums. *Cold turkey*, built over an unremittently driving ostinato, is especially significant in this context, for it's a song of frenzied despair ('I'm in at the deep freeze') which is also an appeal for salvation ('Get me out of this hell'). There's a specific relationship to the Mummy cycle of the first solo LP, for the words say 'I wish I was a baby, I wish I was dead . . . O I'll be a good boy, please make me well'; and the hammering ostinato and imprisoning tritone (A natural to E flat) are hardly less savage than the comparable passages that occur – at the identical pitch too – in the later songs. That there's a link between this elemental quality and Yoko's own musical explorations is evident in the two Yoko numbers that fill the other side of the disc – *Live peace in Toronto 1969* – that includes *Cold turkey*. The first, *Don't worry Kyoko, Mummy's only looking for her hand in the snow*, is basically a Lennonesque rock number, though it has no obvious 'tune', and is yowled and howled by Yoko in her beast and bird-like, mainly wordless ululation. Perhaps because the rock quality gives the gibbering urgency and direction, Yoko can follow this piece with *John, John, let's hope for peace*, which is a summation of her brand of aural Primal Therapy. In the context of John's music her moans and groans, whimpers, shudders and ultimately screams around John's name attain a cumulative intensity over an electrophonic drone that gradually and remorselessly engulfs consciousness. Thus concentrated, Yoko's variety of vocal resource seems almost as expressive as Ornette Coleman's instrumentalism; though 'beyond' Time, the piece is not too long to avoid enervating repetition. The effect, with its microtonal distortions of pitch, is ritualistic and non-Western, if not specifically oriental. The ritual of Primal Therapy is of its nature private, even when enacted, as it was in Toronto, before a vast crowd. Certainly the piece is powerfully disturbing and in no sense phoney. There can be little doubt that John's response to such music helped him to come to terms with the violence within himself, if not exactly to triumph over it. Yoko showed him that – as he put it in one of the later songs – it won't hurt you 'to feel your own pain'.

A note on Paul and Linda

The liaison and ultimate marriage of John, the wild and way-out one, with the avant-garde artist and Inscrutable Oriental was bound to make the headlines, with or without John's and Yoko's connivance. The disturbance the marriage created complements the near-psychotic disturbance in John's personality; and brought into the open biographically it released latent artistic potential. Paul's marriage to Linda, on the other hand, hasn't ruffled any waters; it seems to have been assumed that, after his sportive adolescence, he has 'settled down' with a nice girl and nice kids, creating an idyllic domesticity in a (however lavishly equipped?) country retreat. We don't know how far this account squares with hard facts: *is* Linda nice, are the kids delightful, does the rural domesticity warm the heart? What's interesting, however, is that such questions are not asked. Paul's biography, as contrasted with John's, seems insignificant: which may merely mean that unequivocally good news is not News.

Yoko helped John to discover or rediscover his 'deeper' self. If Linda hasn't done the same for Paul the reason may be that there is no deeper layer of experience to be revealed. None the less, Linda has clearly played a part in Paul's solo work, and this part is increasingly important or, at least, accredited. The sleeve of the first solo disc informed us that 'vocals and instrumentals' were by Paul, 'harmonies' (whatever that may mean) by Linda; on the sleeve of *Ram* Linda makes the grade as joint composer. Now (March 1972) Paul has formed a new group under the title of Wings, in which Linda is designated joint composer and producer, as well as being responsible for minor matters like photography. It's not yet clear what future is planned for the group which has so far made mainly sporadic, *ad hoc* public appearances, without commercial promotion. The character of the group is, however, unambiguous. Paul's highly professional musicianship combines with Linda's unpretentious amateurism and with two musicians who are halfway between amateur and pro, for Paul picked up drummer Denny Seiwell and guitarist Denny Laine on the periphery of the showbiz world. So between them Paul the professional, Linda the amateur, and the two Denny's who might be described as technically virtuosic folk musicians develop the innocent sophistication or sophisticated innocence which had always been a hallmark of Paul's work. The music comes out as countrified, even old-world and nostalgically Edenic: which may be an evasion of the rock-bottom reality sought for by John, yet may also have a positive aspect in that its celebration of the milder simplicities corresponds to an inarticulate need of today's young. Though violence and anguish may plumb deeper, good humour, even cosiness, is not necessarily false.

The first disc issued by the new group Wings is called *Wild Life*, and it's interesting that the title song should be a conservation number: we must save the birds and beasts if we're to have any hope of saving ourselves. While the piece hasn't much musical substance, consisting of a modally ululating lament over a simple descending ostinato, the thinness of the material is essential to its cumulative effect, and the music, with its antiphonally choric refrains, gathers a quality of gentle grandeur. In the light of this the countrified happiness of a child's runic incantation such as *Bip bop* acquires an unexpected resonance: as does a simple love song such as *I am your singer*. Here the tune is sung by Linda in a style that makes no claim to technical expertise, not even that of the virtuosic folk artist; yet the instrumental playing is brilliant, not excluding the naïve recorders, so the song's faintly disturbing quality comes from our recognition that it isn't quite what it seems. Similarly *Love is strange* – which simply reiterates the fact that love is strange, though some people 'take it for a game' – creates a sense of child-like *wonder*, as well as hedonistic pleasure, from its fusion of (amateur) lyrical innocence with (professional) rhythmic and textural sensitivity, even complexity. This reminds us of an early Beatle song, being at once happy and precarious. Paul's *Tomorrow* – a love song which is also an *appeal* for faith – likewise combines elemental, folk-like simplicity in its fine, rather grandly sad modal tune, with high technical expertise in the rhythmic, harmonic and textural subtleties of the guitar playing. The skill doesn't discredit the simplicity; it rather tells us that to achieve such directness here and now is a task calling for both delicacy in emotional response and also for considerable toughness – the coda grows unexpectedly powerful, even unpretentiously heroic.

Though a song such as this may be a slighter achievement than John's recent discs, it certainly doesn't come out as merely muzak to my ears, as it does to John's. Some of the numbers on *Wild Life* may be directly related to songs on John's two solo LPs, and the parallels are fascinating and revealing. Thus *Mumbo* is a voodoo piece, imaginative in its use of electronic organ, startlingly virtuosic in its drumming; but whereas John's *Well, well, well* and *I don't wanna be a soldier* are voodoo ceremonies in nightmare, Paul's mumbo-jumbo is grotesquely comic. This means he's less involved in the frenzy, not having suffered it; but it doesn't reduce the experience to parody. Two songs – *Some*

people never know and *Dear friend* – offer oblique answers to
John's anti-Paul tirade which had asked How do you sleep at
night? For *Some people* suggests that some can sleep, others
can't and the moral rights and wrongs of sleeping or not sleeping
shouldn't be given *a priori* answers. The song's slow rumba
rhythm questions, yet assuages. Similarly *Dear friend* asks What's
the time, is it really the borderline, did it really mean so much to
you, are you afraid? – in a sad modal tune involving repeated notes,
over a rigid rhythmic ostinato, with phrases separated by lengthy
pauses: all of which effects are found in John's anti-Paul song.
Occasionally Paul's song teeters on the brink of farce, as the
tune wings him into extravagant falsetto; but this element of
danger intensifies rather than diminishes the song's almost-noble
austerity, and its emotional weight seems the more impressive
after the unpretentious character of the previous songs. Significantly – even though he finally deflates it with a distorted
fragment of instrumental music comparable with the trumpery
coda to *The end* of *Abbey Road* – Paul places this song last on
the disc. It would seem that between John and Paul the sparks
still fly; and that even in separation and mutual hostility they still
need one another as impetus to their finest work.

8. Elegy on a Mythology

This has been a book about Beatle songs – verse and music: about which little has been written. About the Beatles as a social phenomenon many thousands of words have been uttered, and I don't propose to add many to them. The Beatles' songs, after all, are what remains when the hubbub has subsided, and in the not so long run the songs are what the Beatles 'represent'. Indeed, since it's music that is the real meaning of the myth, I must end with an enquiry into the relationship between the two.

The Beatles' 'significance', as a part of social history, is inseparable from the ambiguity of their function. As pop musicians they are simultaneously magicians (dream-weavers), priests (ritual celebrants), entertainers (whiling away empty time), and artists (incarnating and reflecting the feelings – rather than thoughts – and perhaps the conscience of a generation). If this multiplicity of function is a source of much semantic confusion, both on the part of the Beatles themselves and of those who comment on them, it is also a source of their strength: as will be evident if we discuss each aspect in turn and in relationship to the others. Thus the magical aspects of Beatle music, on which we have commented from their earliest songs to the Magical Mystery Tour itself, answer precisely to Collingwood's definition: 'Magic is a representation where the emotion evoked is an emotion valued on account of its function in practical life, evoked in order that it may discharge that function, and fed by the generative or focusing magical life into the practical life that needs it. Magical activity is a kind of dynamo supplying the mechanism of practical life with the emotional current that drives it. Hence magic is a necessity for every sort and condition of man, and is actually found in every healthy society. A society which thinks, as our own thinks, that it has outlived the need of magic, is either mistaken in that opinion, or else it is a dying society, perishing for lack of interest in its own maintenance.' Those words of Collingwood were written in 1937 when magic, in western civilisation, seemed to survive only in degraded form in weddings, funerals, and sports such as fox-hunting and cricket. Between then and now pop in general and the Beatles in particular have reinstated magic; and it won't do for self-righteous guardians of 'civilisation' and tradition to maintain that the rediscovery of magic has *merely* unleashed forces of destruction.

This takes us from the magical to the priestly function of Beatle music. In their early years all Beatle music was also dance; and as Susanne Langer has put it, 'all sorts of puzzling dance forms and practices, origins, connections with other arts, and relations to magic and religion, become clear as soon as one conceives the dance to be neither plastic art nor music, nor a presentation of story, but a play of Powers made visible'. Or as Curt Sachs has said: 'In the ecstasy of the dance man bridged the chasm between this and the other world, to the realm of demons, spirits, and God.' In the magic circle of the dance (to quote Langer again) 'all daemonic powers are loosed. The mundane realm is excluded, and with it, very often, the restrictions and proprieties that belong to it.' 'Ecstasy' is nothing but the feeling of entering such a realm; and only in a very partial sense can we dismiss the teenager's orgiastic dancing as a tipsy escape from the hard realities of life. On the contrary, as compared with the romantic unreality of the previous generation's ballroom dancing (which is in turn related to the fairy-tale myth of classical ballet), one might rather describe teenage dance as practical and functional in Collingwood's sense; an inchoate attempt to rediscover the springs of being. For the 'individual dancer dances not so much with his fellows – they are all transformed into dance-beings, or even into mere parts of a dynamic organism – as he dances with the world; he dances with the music, with his own voice . . . with light, and rain, and earth'. Pop music and dance have no truck with the separation of the dance as spectacle from the dance as activity, in which 'the audience participates by singing, and sometimes clapping, stamping and jigging' and screaming. This goes along with 'fairly crude face-painting, artificially altered eyebrows, dyed finger and toe nails, etc; a strong tendency to myth and cult activity in political life;

and a return to all-out tribal soldiery instead of the more special-
ised reliance on professional armies that had allowed seventeenth-
and eighteenth-century Europe to develop an essentially civil
culture.' The magical and priestly primitivism of Beatle (and other
pop) music is basic, not bogus; its implications cannot be glibly
effaced. Like black jazz, it's a release of sexual aggression in
ritualisation, even a redirection of aggression to creative ends; it
has often been noted that a pop group session bears many similari-
ties to what Durkheim has called the 'effervescent' phase of a
revivalist cult.

Mary Douglas, in her book *Natural Symbols*, has reminded us
that in revivalist movements 'emotions run high, formalism of all
kinds is denounced, the favoured patterns of religious worship
include trance or glossalalia, trembling, shaking, or other ex-
pressions of incoherence and dissociation. Differentiation is
deplored. The movement is seen to be universal in potential
membership. Generally the stage of effervescence gives way to
various forms of sectarianism . . . But it is not quite true that
effervescence must either be routinized or fizzle out. It is possible
for it to be sustained indefinitely as the normal form of worship.
The only requirement is that the level of social organization be
sufficiently low and the pattern of roles sufficiently unstructured'.
This is why pop cults are also 'a form of protest against resented
forms of social control', epitomised in the contrast of smooth with
shaggy hair. Since the Beatles' heyday pop musicians have
increasingly developed into Calibans or bearded Prophets, 'who
tend to be shaggy, unkempt individuals . . . who arise in peripheral
areas of society. They express in their bodies the independence
of social norms which their peripheral origins inspire in them.
It is no accident that St. John the Baptist lived in the desert and
wore skins, or that Nuer prophets wear beards and long hair in a
fashion that ordinary Nuer find displeasing. Everywhere, social
peripherality has the same physical forms of expression, bizarre
and untrimmed . . . How shaggy can they get? What are the limits
of shagginess and bodily abandon?'

The parallels between the pop phenomenon and the revivalist
cult are genuine enough; and there is a still more specific relation-

ship to a Greek Dionysiac ritual. Indeed I have related my account
of the Beatles' musical evolution to the successive stages of a
Dionysiac initiation ceremony through which – with a fusion of
classical and Christian mythology – the young are rediscovering
the reality of sex both as god and as devil. Whilst this comparison
is seriously intended there is also, of course, an element of irony,
if not facetiousness, within it, since the magical-priestly properties
of Beatle (and other pop) music can be only latent, or at most
emergent: for they and we were born into a society not in fact
dominated by magic and ritual, but by entertainment and art.
The magical-religious and the art-entertainment functions of
Beatle music don't cancel one another out; they do, however, in
their interrelationship, contain an element of equivocation: which
is part of the Beatles' 'representative' fascination.

   R. G. Collingwood, in the justly famous book on aesthetics
from which I have already quoted, distinguishes amusement (or
entertainment) from magic in these terms: 'An amusement is a
device for the discharge of emotions in such a way that they shall
not interfere with the concerns of practical life. . . . The artist as a
purveyor of amusement makes it his business to please his audience
by arousing certain emotions in them and providing them with a
make-believe situation in which these emotions can be harmlessly
discharged. The experience of being amused is sought not for the
sake of anything to which it stands as a means, but for its own
sake. Hence, while magic is utilitarian, amusement is not utilitarian
but hedonistic. The work of art, so called, which provides the
amusement is, on the contrary, strictly utilitarian. Unlike a work
of art proper, it has no value in itself; it is simply a means to an
end.' Thus 'entertainment' offers substitutes for experience:
pornography is a simulation of sex, the horror story a simulation
of fear, both affording titillation without commitment or threat.
Whatever art is – and this is not the place to embark on aesthetics –
it is not simulation but creation; and what is created are 'symbolic
forms', abstracts of reality variously and complexly related to the
artist's own experience. In fact, though art is intrinsically 'beyond'
entertainment, magic and ritual, there can never be clearly defined
barriers between them, and the belief that entertainment as escape

and art as truth must be mutually opposed has been fostered only because, in our industrial society, the techniques of the machine have made the prostitution of feeling so easy and so devastatingly effective. The tie-up between art, entertainment and advertising introduces the red herring of the profit motive; to assume that material success must mean a betrayal of artistic truth is at once a gross over-simplification and an under-estimation of the forces of the unconscious.

This is why both the Beatles themselves and their critics talk such juvenile drivel when they try to rationalise the Beatle experience. Since the Beatles are a product of the pop music industry – the account runs – the only 'reality' must be the profit-motive. John has called himself a conman, like Beethoven (a conversation between Lennon and Beethoven on the subject would be worth hearing), and at one time declared that his songs are totally meaningless. Clearly this cannot apply to his recent, almost therapeutically autobiographical solo albums, which may entertain, though entertainment is no longer their reason for existing. One may doubt, however, whether the Beatles have ever really meant their more cynically trivialising pronouncements: for if with one breath they've denied that their music has any meaning beyond its (extremely effective) money making properties, with the next breath they've said they know they're not verbally articulate, but don't need to be, since 'talking is the slowest form of communicating. Music is much better. We're communicating to the outside world through our music.' The probity of the Beatles' technique, on which we've commented *passim*, is relevant here. Their verses function effectively as words for music, using the language of common speech, occasionally blossoming into poetry through the unusual collocation of apparently commonplace details; both in their down-to-earth concision and in their English zaniness (their closest antecedent is surely Edward Lear) they're poles apart from the simplistic gobbledegook that characterises the 'poetry' of so much progressive pop. Similarly, their music shows an impeccable adjustment of means to ends, achieving its subtlest effects by the simplest procedures. Even in their later, more experimental days Beatle songs never go on too long. They

have, of course, their weaker moments, but they seldom outstay
their welcome. Again the contrast with much progressive pop is
pointed; the Beatles' superiority is inseparable from an entirely
intuitive self-knowledge.

Looking back, one can perhaps see the Beatles' tie-up with the
world of commerce, if not as a positive asset, at least as an essential
part of their intuitive reality. The leery laugh at the end of *Within
you without you* may be self-defensive trivialisation; but George
simply says 'after all that long Indian stuff you want some light
relief. It's a relief after five minutes of sad music. You haven't
got to take it all that seriously, you know. . . . It's true, but it's
still a joke . . . It's serious and it's not serious.' This seems to me
perhaps the truest and most touching quality of Beatle music, and
the quality that makes their work so sensitively attuned to their
generation. The young are wary and won't, if they can help it,
once more be taken in. At the same time they're not hard-boiled;
and their search for whatever salvation there may be, by whatever
means, however confused, springs from the heart.

It's in this sense that the Beatles' biographies, and their methods
of work, have some slight relevance to their music and mythology.
Through their music they rendered articulate a generation that
was, through no fault of its own, pitifully bemused and befuddled;
and they couldn't have done this but for their extraordinary
ordinariness. Ringo really came from a terraced house in Liverpool's dockland; his parents were very poor, and parted when he
was three. He suffered two serious illnesses when a child, had little
formal education, never took the eleven plus examination, and had
no experience of music until the skiffle craze. Ringo seems to have
taken all this quietly: unlike John, whose parents also separated
when he was a baby, leaving him to be reared by his aunt Mimi,
whose affectionate conventionality fanned, rather than quashed,
John's rebelliousness. As he approached his teens his mother
Julia came back into his life and he established with her a relationship of some intensity, identifying with her as (unlike Mimi) a
groovy one. She laughed at his wild jokes; and played the banjo!
Julia's death in a car accident, when John was seventeen, made him
very savage. Clearly he fantasised over her in later life; was cruel

to his girls; reinvoked her in his son, Julian; objectified his near-psychotic relation to her in the *Plastic Ono Band* solo LP.

George is the only Beatle to come from a fairly normal domestic background. His father was a bus conductor and later driver, his mother a Catholic who raised a large family. Mrs. Harrison's ardent Catholicism may have initiated George's religious bent; yet, though without John's powerful personality and native intelligence, he too was a rebel and the first Beatle to sport, like the god Dionysus, 'luxuriant hair'. He went to the same school as Paul, whose mother was also a Catholic and whose father was a salesman who at one time ran a small dance band. Paul was the only Beatle to achieve a measure of conventional success at grammar school. He was the 'keeny' who became the Beatles' PR man in the early days: though the artistic promotion was as much, or more, John's as his. Paul's mother died of cancer at the age of 45, so his home background too was disrupted. Compared with John's and Ringo's, however, it could be called stable.

It must have been evident, early on, that John was an exceptional person; that Paul was bright and had talents; that George had latent potential; that Ringo had a humorous fortitude. No one could have guessed, however, at what was to come from the evidence of their first years, when there were five Beatles – John, Paul, George, Pete Best and Stu Sutcliffe, but no Ringo. The music from the Hamburg days, now reissued on an LP, has the charm of its puerility, but puerile it is, in every sense. Sutcliffe, apparently an intelligent and talented youth and, like John, an art student, died tragically of a brain tumour; Pete Best was deposed, in slightly dubious circumstances, in favour of Ringo, and relapsed into obscurity, missing out on fame and fortune. Perhaps it was providential that the Beatles, having found ordinary Ringo, discovered too the extraordinariness that made them legendary. They started as folk-artists in that they worked empirically, teaching one another guitar chords, with Paul or George always a few chords ahead; inventing their originally insignificant lyrics as a sort of rhyming game; creating 'talismantic' refrains by a process of 'instant vocalisation'. Yet to deplore the illiteracy of the Beatles – or of any pop or jazz group – is nonsensical: for the essence of their achievement is that it is a return from literate and visual to aural and oral culture.

Indeed black music came to obsess white youth precisely because it fused two elements that seem to be contradictory but are not. Jazz was something done, acted out, not passively experienced; and usually the acting out involved a game and a contest. But it was also honest, non-escapist, oral, unassimilable by our technological society, and therefore of its instinctive nature a protest. 'Blues combines the immediacy of speech with the passion of song', Ben Sidron has said; and the band jazz of New Orleans was 'created by both performer and audience in constant interaction, an exchange of faith not unlike that of the preacher-congregation relationship or that of voodoo ritual'. The physicality of the (later) shouting blues singer aimed at a personal ecstasy that also embraced audience or tribe; similarly Beatle performances, in the days when they appeared in public, encouraged immediate involvement in *things as they happen*. Syntactical logic is irrelevant; what matters is the game we're playing and the feeling it celebrates, at the given moment. This is why the music, made up by people who couldn't read notation, had to be in part improvised, in part aurally memorised; and is why instrumental techniques had to be directly derived from the movements of hands and body, singing techniques derived from an instinctive orality, like that of the black soul singer whose black music had become internationally a voice for white youth. It's interesting that, even after the Beatles had become technically sophisticated and had relinquished public performance, they still preserved, in their approach to composition, an element of play: in which respect they are returning to one of the basic origins of art which Western civilisation, in its hyper-self-consciousness, had come near to forgetting. We speak, after all, of 'playing' music; language is of its nature metamorphical, and every metaphor is a play upon words. Children's play, according to Erik Erikson, is an 'infantile form of the human ability to deal with experience by creating moral situations and to master reality by experiment'; and still deeper is the desire to effect a magic act, a temporary suspension of normal life for the sacred session of play. As Huizinga has said in *Homo Ludens*, play is a free activity outside ordinary life, not 'serious' in the sense that it implies practical responsibilities, yet intensely solemn in that it involves the player, within rigidly proscribed rules, utterly. Games are played without regard for practical ends; within strict boundaries of time and place (the magic line or circle); and often with disguise ('dressing up') to separate the in-group from the common world. As Huizinga points out, the word illusion derives from *in lusio*, or in play.

So children's games, even in our modern industrial communities, always involve an element of 'entertainment', as an explosion of animal high spirits; an element of illusion, dressing up or make-believe; and an element of ordered body-movement (dance), usually accompanied by song (musical melody), sometimes without words, sometimes with nonsense words, sometimes with language that is meaningful below the level of consciousness. This sounds remarkably like a description of an early Beatle session; and we remember that even in their later days George described his 'long, sad Indian stuff' as being at once 'serious and not serious'. George Martin's descriptions of the Beatles' chaotic sessions in the recording studio still stress the playfulness of this activity. Meeting as folk artists of the global village, the Beatles discovered in the disc itself an extension of oral tradition. In the studio sounds are discovered by experiment and exploration, even by processes analogous to the folk contest, riddle and guessing game, the wax disc giving a kind of permanence to what was, in process of creation, transitory and mutable. Thus a chance remark, an idiot catch-phrase, or a snippet of odd or crazy news culled from the papers, from advertisements or wayside graffiti could trigger off a lyric. In the weird spiritual limbo of the Abbey Road studios the Beatles transmuted the flotsam and jetsam of the electronic age into a semi-automatic poetry: just as in their earliest youth they had metamorphosed the semi-articulate clichés of Merseyside lads and lasses. The music too was evolved by trial and error; as John would cap a line by Paul (or vice versa) with a cunning half rhyme, so tunes would be tried out on guitar or piano, altered and amended *ad hoc*, variously scored and rescored, with or without electronic treatment. Each composing Beatle usually took the lead in his own song, but Paul, as the keeny and perhaps the most musically expert, was the readiest with advice. Though George Martin himself had the technical know-how the Beatles lacked, he doesn't regard himself as more than intermediary. Paul, for instance, sang and mimed the famous trumpet interlude in *Penny Lane* and the horn obbligato in *For no one;* John was usually vaguer about his intentions, but knew unambiguously when things were right; George was always responsible for his own numbers. This machine-age folk empiricism sometimes produced inspired effects by accident, as in the case of *Strawberry fields*, which was tried out in two versions, one much slower than the other and in a different key. John wanted part of one, part of the other; Martin discovered that by speeding up the slower version and slackening the quicker one they could be brought not only into the same tempo, but also into the same key, though with an odd vacuum-cleaner-like distortion. Such phenomena are part of the 'aural mythology' of the LP disc, which creates a sound-environment. *Playing* around with the controls is, indeed, part of the experience. I suspect, for instance, that the extraordinary between-sleeping-and-waking effect of the instrumental parts in John's *I'm only sleeping* was created by reversed double-tracking; and it has been suggested that that strange baby-voice in which John sings *Lucy in the sky* could have been maintained only by way of a preliminary inhaling of helium.

In so far as they remained empiricists, the Beatles were folk heroes; in so far as they were representative of electronic age man they were metamorphosed into gods – as John said, quite literally if momentarily more influential than Jesus Christ. In an apotheosis of democracy, the Beatles were deified for their extraordinary ordinariness. All over the world girls dedicated their lives to Beatle-worship, fainted in droves at their performances. Not merely the young, but the ancient, the maimed, the crippled, fought savagely to touch the magic Beatle forelock, the hem of the sacred coat, many believing that a miraculous cure was feasible. So in their lives these gods were swirled willy-nilly out of *this* world, and their obsession first with the drug experience, then with the Maharishi, was for them – as for the young in general – in part a search for escape from routine normality, in part an attempt to habituate themselves to a fabulous world beyond their, or any common man's, comprehension. The Beatles' experiments with drugs thus have similar motivation to the jazzman's of the previous generation, though both the motivation and the expression of it were less radical, since white youth, though disabused, wasn't irrevocably up against it; LSD produces visions and nightmares, but is not suicidal, as was Charlie Parker's heroin. Similarly the Beatles' tinkering with oriental metaphysics, even if 'sincere', as was certainly the case with George, hardly amounts to more than an alleviatory game if contrasted with, say, the Indian influence in the late music of John Coltrane, who might genuinely be said to have prayed with and through his horn. For the Beatles, indeed, LSD and the Maharishi were an experience they went through in order to deal with the lunacy of their global village lives, which corporately destroyed them utterly, and came near to destroying them as individuals. Miraculously, however, their music was not destroyed. On the contrary, the more they were drawn into the wide, wild world of commerce and conmen, of hypnosis and hysteria, of bestiality and bastardy ('the Beatles were all bastards', John has said), the more – perhaps compensatorily – their music penetrated into, and preserved, the heart's truth. Through their still innocent music they came back to confront the problems of human relationships, here and now, in the ordinary, if no longer Liverpudlian, world.

So, in terms of music, John has returned, again and again, to basic hard rock and blues, in which he finds what he calls 'first person music' ('It's me! And nobody else. That's why I like it. It's real, that's all.'). Paul has returned to corny ballad and country music ('Me – I'm conservative. I feel a need to check things. I was the last to try pot and LSD and floral clothes. I'm slower than John.'). George has returned to the Gospel hymn orientalised ('Reaching a blissful state is the most important thing, but I've still got a job to do, being a Beatle.'). Ringo, with fame and fortune, goes on drumming away with the solo Beatles, happy with wife and kids and the telly ('I'm best really with my hands. I can do most little jobs if I'm just left on my own. It's when things are written down I'm no good.'). So in a sense the words of Ringo have remained true until the end: 'we're unassuming, unaffected, and British to the core.' John's famous crack at the Royal Command Performance – 'those in the cheap seats may clap; the rest should rattle their jewellery' – is dead on the mark; and although one might maintain that they shouldn't have accepted their M.B.E.s, having accepted them it was inevitable that, waiting in the Palace, they should giggle. 'We collapsed, the whole thing was so funny. There was this Guardsman telling us how to march, how many steps, and how to curtsey when we met the Queen. We knew in our hearts she was just some woman, yet we were going through with it. We'd agreed to it . . . I always hated all the social things. All the horrible events and presentations we had to go to. All false. You could see right through them all. . . . Perhaps it was partly from class. No it wasn't. It was because they really *were* all false.'

'All that business,' John has also said, 'it was awful, it was fucking humiliation. One has to completely humiliate oneself to be what the Beatles were, and that's what I resent. I didn't know, I didn't foresee. It happened bit by bit, gradually, until this complete craziness is surrounding you, and you're doing exactly what you don't want to do with people you can't stand – the people you hated when you were ten' . . . 'One of my big things is that I wish to be a fisherman. I know it sounds silly – and I'd sooner be rich than poor and the rest of all that shit – but I wish that pain was ignorance or bliss or something. If you don't know, man, then there's no pain' . . . 'People are so aggressive . . . I need to have a look at the grass. I'm always writing about my English garden. I need the trees and the grass.' John's autobiographical solo albums bring all this, at last, into the open; and help to explain why, at the climax of the Beatles' career, when decorations were showered upon them and Beatle mums were opening church fêtes, Beatle music remained a paradox, vulnerable yet incorruptible throughout the horrendous circumstances of their deified lives – about which one may read in the immense accumulation of peripheral information and misinformation. Most of this is totally irrelevant to what the Beatles have created in their music: except that their achievement wouldn't be so heroic had they not suffered as scapegoats and sacrificial victims for us all. The Beatles' lives enacted out the rape of commerce and the electronic media upon us; whilst their music remained as true as truth's simplicity – with the understanding that today's simplicity cannot avoid manifold ironies and ambiguities. They're not, after all, gods with feet of clay; they're young men who have made songs meaningful for their generation and for us all. If they guffaw at 'intellectuals' (like me) who discover 'hidden meanings' in their songs, they've given plenty of evidence that they really know that these meanings are not hidden at all but merely, like eighty per cent of the meaning in all art, in part unconscious. 'Standing for' us, they are folk musicians of the global village who, individaully if not corporately, have (just) come through.

In spite of the commercial stresses, in spite of the lapses into infantile narcissism and into pseudo-mystical twaddle, the Beatles – along with a few other flowers of pop – have occasionally reawakened our ritual sense; and we have to see this phenomenon in relationship to comparable developments in all the arts at all levels, remembering that the public for late Beatles and progressive pop overlaps with that for Stockhausen, Cage, Partch, Berio, even perhaps Tippett's ritual operas and Britten's 'parables for church performance'. That the Beatles, unlike the phenomena listed above, were a cult involving millions of young people is part of their importance: which is not to be diminished by a glib reference to the young's new economic viability. It is rather that such music youthfully demonstrates how man's life, in the words of Octavio Paz, is 'ceasing to be a spatial measurement and changing into a source, a spring, in the absolute present'. Pop has reasserted the spirit of fiesta which, whether secular or religious, allows us, momently released from Time, to 'emerge from our solitude and become one with creation': as were the 'mature' Beatles when they made the affirmation, however ambiguous, of *The end*; as had been the boy Beatles when they wonderingly piped 'I saw her standing there'; as were we ourselves when, as children, chanting 'wallflowers, wallflowers', we mythologised the act and fact of dying, even in the spring of the year.

Postscript

Since this book was completed a small amount of additional recorded material has been issued. Since the John and Yoko double album *Some time in New York City* to some degree modifies the view I've given of his recent work, I append a notice of the discs which I contributed to the *New Statesman* of 27 October 1972:

In their glorious hey-day the Beatles were a foursome that created a communal mythology of the young, pertinent and potent because their songs also sprang from individualised experience. John and Paul, the two leading Beatle composers, were complementary not in the sense that they composed together – after the early days they seldom did – but because they were opposite poles that generated electrical sparks that in turn fired and flamed. Now that they're separate, but still creating, we can see more clearly what each offered; and can also realise how difficult it is for one to function without the other. McCartney, with his new group Wings, produces pleasant songs more than competently executed; though they sometimes have topical themes such as conservation or pollution, they're turned outward to the world, seldom emotionally involved. With Lennon's first solo LP, on the other hand, personal involvement was everything, for the songs were directly autobiographical and an extension of the primal therapy which John and Yoko had recently undergone. In infantile hysteria John yelled for the lost maternal breast, yet in the process obliterated the Mother and struck the Father dead. None the less, his personal frenzy was metamorphosed into rudimentary art: into the young white blues of affluence and possession, as against the old black blues of poverty and dispossession; and the integrity of his "British blues" technique – both in composition and in style of performance – was strong enough to allow his pain to "stand for" that of the urban young everywhere.

On his second solo LP, *Imagine*, it seemed that he would be able to build on this personal catharsis, for the autobiographical elements, though still powerful, were less obtrusive, and the total effect of the still-savage songs was curiously and courageously affirmative. Interestingly enough, this was most impressively manifest in the big new-voodoo song of negation *I don't wanna be a soldier*, and in the explicitly anti-McCartney number *How do you sleep at night*. To have achieved this tough maturity must have called for considerable spiritual stamina; that it couldn't be long sustained was hardly surprising. In any case, it isn't sustained on the new double album *Some time in New York City* (Apple PCSP 716); for here John relinquishes personal experience in favour of the easier option of the public gesture. As William Blake and the earlier Beatles knew, generalities signify only in relation to particularities; and for the particularities of the first two Lennon solo LPs the political themes of *Some time in New York City* are no adequate substitute. There's a hint of the former interior energy in the women's lib. song *Woman is the nigger of the world*; but the opening phrase, which has the tension of true jazz and stimulates some fine instrumental soloing, eventually dissipate in ramble and repetition, and in harmonic shifts that cease to surprise because the tune lacks direction. The more successful songs, such as the Irish troubles number *Sunday bloody Sunday*, come off more through the remorselessness of their violence and the sheer decibel content of its presentation than through musical character or quality. Other songs rely on other extra-musical means, such as a presumably ironic contrast between the grim glumness of the words and the obvious corn of the music; thus John's *The luck of the Irish* verbally demolishes the beastly English to a music-hall tune that is all lyrical blarney, whilst Yoko's *We're all water* – verbally the closest approach to wit and poetry on the disc – also works, rather effectively, the same way. But I don't know what to make of her *Sisters O sisters*, for if the mind-boggling triteness of the tune is a joke against utopianism we're left with utter nihilism, whereas if it isn't intended ironically I can only be glad that I'm unlikely to survive to taste the "new world it's never too late to build". There's a difference between what's simple and what's moronic. On the two earlier discs John's subjective infantilism was a process of painful self-discovery – for himself, for today's young, and vicariously for ourselves. On this disc undifferentiated rage on behalf of all radical causes spends itself in thin air; and political – unlike personal – infantilism, since it cannot be psychologically transcended, is as dangerous as it is ineffective.

The companion disc, *Live Jam*, is – in the light of Lennon's earlier achievements – even more depressing that *Some time in New York City*. Here there are no political gestures; but what we're left with, in live, mostly improvised performance, is little more than a public scream. Since the screamers include people as talented as Lennon and Zappa (and Yoko has yelled well enough from time to time), there are bound to be some interesting noises on and off. Self-indulgence could hardly be carried further, however, since to *this* infantilism there is neither artistic catharsis nor passionate (if intellectually half-based and musically irrelevant) political conviction. Compositional silence and social-political action is presumably the next step, for Lennon as for some representatives of music's avant-garde. Let's hope it will be more responsible than these discs suggest.

Glossary

acciaccatura in eighteenth-century music a very rapid, dissonant grace or decorative note approaching the main note. Though the term comes from polite music, acciaccaturas are by nature congenial to folk and jazz guitar, adding a percussive sharpness to the attack: hence their relevance to Beatle music.

added sixth the chord consisting of the major triad with the sixth degree of the scale added (e.g. C, E, G, A).

aeolian mode represented on the piano by the scalewise sequence of tones beginning on A: so the mode has minor third, flat sixth and flat seventh.

African when I use this word I mean it, and am not employing it as a synonym for American Negro. The primitivism of early Beatle music is often startlingly similar to that of some African children's musics, and this is a comment on the nature of their experience. It does not, of course, imply that the Beatles had heard African children's musics and were imitating them, as they imitated the Negro blues.

antiphony a responsorial technique whereby, in primitive musics, the singing leader is chorically answered by the tribe. Antiphony happens between the Negro preacher and his congregation also; and in more sophisticated form between the Catholic or Anglican priest and his choir and/or congregation.

appoggiatura a dissonant note added to a concord, on to which it resolves. Whilst it's usually thought of in association with eighteenth-century (classical baroque) music, it's a natural fact of the language of music, more or less synonymous with the sigh: a point of tension which is then relaxed. The dissonant tone which resolves on to consonance is found in all musics, everywhere, dissonance and consonance being scientific criteria referring to the relatively complex or simple vibration ratios existing between tones.

The best way to experience this is for two people to sing the same tone; one moves up a semitone whilst the other stays still; the upper voice then falls, or resolves, on to the original note. The meaning of the terms tension and relaxation, in relation to aural experience, will then be almost physically evident.

arpeggio   the notes of a chord 'spread out' in linear sequence.

barrelhouse music   a 'low' instrumental form of the blues usually played, in bars and brothels, on piano.

blues and blue notes   the classic form of the American Negro's poetry and music. Originally blues were sung to guitar accompaniment, the melodic and to some extent the rhythmic techniques being derived from African folk sources, whilst the harmonic and metrical structure came from the white hymn and march. The basic form consists of four bars of tonic; two bars of subdominant plus two of tonic; one bar of subdominant plus one bar of dominant plus two bars of tonic: though since blues structure is empirical there are many variations on the pattern. The point lies, anyway, in the tension between the rigidity of White harmony and metre and the flexibility and freedom of Black melody and rhythm, neither of which are fully notable in white, Western terms. References to the blues usually apply more to the folk characteristics of the music than to its strict formal properties; blue notes are by no means restricted to the blues (cf. false relation).

boogie   an instrumental form of the blues, usually for piano or guitar, and usually fairly fast. The boogie is an obsessively driving figure, usually in the bass, repeated as an ostinato, often in dotted rhythm (umtee umtee).

cadence   the harmonic close to a composition or section of one, usually moving from dominant chord to tonic (perfect cadence) or from subdominant to tonic (plagal cadence). The perfect cadence, as its name implies, is the most final; the plagal cadence says Amen. Imperfect cadences, or half closes, work the other way round: from tonic to dominant or subdominant. They mark pauses, ends of phrases; but never the end of a whole.

chromatic   scalewise movement entirely by semitones; hardly found outside Western music, for the division of the octave into equal semitones has no root in acoustical facts. Not surprisingly, Beatle music is never chromatic though they occasionally take over chromatic passing notes and even chromatic harmonies from Western art music.

coda   literally a tailpiece. In the pop standard, and in many Beatle songs, the coda often repeats material from the middle section.

da capo   a recapitulation of the first strain, after the 'middle'. The da capo or sandwich form in the pop standard is the same as the Italian eighteenth-century aria da capo form, though the material may be simpler.

diminished seventh   a chord consisting of superimposed minor thirds (e.g. F sharp, A, C, E flat) which, since it incorporates two tritones (see below) is traditionally disruptive.

dominant   the fifth degree of the scale and the key associated with that note: e.g. to C the dominant is G.

dominant seventh   the triad on the dominant with the addition of the seventh degree of the scale, flattened. The chord is especially important in Western music as a means of defining tonality.

dorian mode   on the piano, the scalewise sequence of tones beginning on D, so the mode has flat third, sharp sixth, flat seventh.

drone   a single tone, or possibly two tones, sustained continuously against a moving melodic part. Very common in all folk musics and most oriental music. Best known to us through bagpipe music.

enharmonic   musical puns may be created by the identity, in equal tempered music, between (say) C sharp and D flat; thus the third of a dominant seventh in D might change to the tonic of the remote key of D flat. Such effects aren't common, of course, in music which, like that of the Beatles, is folk-orientated; but they do occur, especially in their later, more sophisticated numbers.

false relation   a clash between the major third, favoured for its harmonic resonance, and the melodic (vocal) minor third. The phenomenon first occurred early in the harmonic era of European music when composers, trained to think vocally and modally, became obsessed with harmonic euphony. Blue notes in American Negro music are a modern example of an exactly comparable phenomenon: white harmony implies the sharp major third, whilst the Negro naturally sings in modal (especially pentatonic) minor thirds; the collision between the two types of thirds is the source of much of the blues' intensity.

flat seventh   the melodic appearance of B flats (say) in what appears to be the key of C major or minor. The terminology is in fact perverse; for the flat seventh is acoustically more 'natural' than the sharp seventh and can be thought of as an oddity only by accepting Western diatonic and tempered scales as the norm: which they are not.

gospel song   a consequence of a fusion of the American Negro's folk heritage and the blues with the Christian hymn. Not clearly distinguishable from the spiritual, though the latter is normally choric whereas the Gospel song may be solo.

heptatonic   the various seven-note modes or scales.

lydian mode   the mode represented by the white notes on the piano, starting from F. The mode is characterised by its disturbingly sharpened fourth; it also has the sharp seventh.

major, minor the two established scale systems of the eighteenth and nineteenth centuries, associated with harmonic tonality. Though the minor form contains survivals of pre-eighteenth-century vocal modality, both major and minor forms exploit sharpened cadential sevenths and call for some system of tempering – the artificial doctoring of pure intervals – to facilitate harmonic development and modulation.

mediant the third degree of the scale and the key associated with that note. Mediant transitions have become prevalent again, along with the modal revival mentioned above, though of course they occur in classical art music too.

melisma (plural **melismata**) an ornamental passage, especially in oriental and medieval music. Strictly speaking, on a single syllable, though the term is loosely used for any decorative twiddle, arabesque or roulade.

microtones, microtonal intervals smaller than a semitone. Not notatable, though very common in oriental music and in all folk melody, including blues and Beatles.

mixolydian mode the sequence of white notes on the piano, beginning on G; thus the mode has sharp third and sharp sixth but flat seventh.

modes, modality, modal the scales in common use before the establishment of the major-minor hierachy. Acoustically derived from the behaviour of the human voice, they naturally predominate in all musics melodically conceived, including folk musics: hence the intuitive return to them in the new, young people's pop. In art music there have been signs of this revival ever since the early years of the century.

modulation movement from one key centre to another; in its strict technical sense applies only to European art music.

Neapolitan cadence in European harmonic music, the approach to the dominant-tonic cadence in the minor key by the

flattened supertonic; i.e. in C, the triad of D flat, followed
by G major with flat seventh, followed by tonic. A highly
emotional intensifying of the cadence, said to have been used
by Neapolitan opera composers to illustrate moments of
extreme stress; later a cliché, though a powerfully effective
one, in classical sonata music.

obbligato a solo part for an instrument, usually in duo with
voice, in baroque and rococo music. The term has been
borrowed and applied to the music of any period.

ostinato an obstinately repeated linear figure or even rhythm,
usually though not necessarily in the bass. The term comes
from art music, though ostinati are of course prevalent in
all primitive musics, in jazz and in pop.

pentatonic the various forms of five-note modes (represented
on the piano by the black notes). Of all scalic formulae the
pentatonic are those most directly derived from the acoustical
facts of the harmonic series: this is why they form the basis
of all primitive musics everywhere, and of most sophisticated
musics that are melodically conceived. The 'modes' (see
above) probably developed as extensions of pentatonicism.
Even today little children, brought up on equal tempered
music, still naturally improvise pentatonic tunes. In their
pentatonicism the Beatles, and other young pop musicians,
are children reborn.

phrygian mode the sequence of white notes on the piano
beginning on E, and thus characterised by flat *second*, third,
sixth and seventh.

plagal cadence the progression from subdominant triad to
tonic (Amen).

portamento in singing a scoop or rapid glissando from one
note to the next. In art song the portamento is a special
(dangerous, often deprecated) effect; but it is very common
and expressive in all folk music and in much oriental music
(which habitually includes microtonal intervals).

relative minor (major) in the European system the minor and major keys that have the same number of sharps and flats.

ritornello in baroque music a short instrumental interlude between the vocal sections of an area or anthem; applied analogically to similar interludes in Beatle music.

rumba rhythm this Latin American dance owes its rhythmic excitation largely to its division of its eight quavers a bar into three plus three plus two: Ta-ta-ta Ta-ta-ta, Ta-ta.

sequence the immediate repetition of a melodic phrase and/or harmonic progression at a different pitch.

sequential seventh rapid but momentary modulations achieved by chains of dominant seventh chords in sequences. Tends to be a prettily sensuous effect, whether in classical baroque music (wherein it was first evolved) or in jazzy pop music before the Second World War.

subdominant the fourth degree of the scale (which is one tone 'under' the fifth or dominant) and the key of that note.

submediant the third below the tonic, which may be minor or major; in the latter case it's called the flat submediant. The *key* of the flat submediant (say A flat to a tonic C) tends to produce a feeling of passive, even luxurious, relaxation: especially in the music of Schubert, who was partial to it. Frequently it has a similar effect in Beatle music.

suspension a note or notes held over, suspended, whilst other, usually lower, parts move, so that dissonance and tension are created in place of concord and euphony. The suspended dissonance then resolves on to consonance, as with an appoggiatura. A technique basic to all music harmonically conceived: and therefore not very important in Beatle music, though when suspensions occur their effect is proportionate to their rarity.

syncopation   a musical syncope, or the missing of a heart-beat:
the accent is displaced from the strong or main beat to (or
fractionally off) the weak beat, producing an effect of excitement or nervosity or both. Although highly developed in
Negro music – it's one of means whereby jazz achieves its
equilibrium between freely singing and dancing line and
imprisoned metrical harmony – syncopation occurs in all
music. Clearly its effect is less patent and potent in music –
such as plainsong and other unaccompanied monodies – in
which no strong metrical beat is evident.

tonality, tonic   strictly speaking, tonality is the relationships
between tones that are inherent in acoustical facts, so that
the term covers all scale systems, or rather formulae, from
the pentatonic to the chromatic. In practice, however,
tonality has become associated with the tempered (major and
minor) scales of European music in the eighteenth and
nineteenth centuries.

triplets   three notes in the time of two.

tritone   the interval of the augmented fourth or diminished
fifth (e.g. B to E sharp or B to F natural). In the Middle
Ages it was known as the *diabolus in musica* because it
devilishly destroyed tonal order, being difficult to sing as a
melodic progression and harmonically inimical to the perfect
fifth (or the perfect fourth which is the fifth inverted). To
medieval people the fifth, being scientifically the most
'perfect' interval after the octave which is hardly a harmony
at all, was a synonym for God. Imperfect fifths or tritones
have preserved their devilish associations throughout the
centuries, down or up to Liszt's and Berlioz's Mephistos,
Vaughan Williams's Satan, and Scriabin's Black Mass
sonata. In some twentieth-century music they perhaps represent a rootless, neutral limbo rather than a destructive force
(Holst's *Egdon Heath*, the last movement of Vaughan
Williams's *Sixth Symphony*); whilst for Messiaen they may
become moments outside Time, since their harmonic root-

lessness means that they do not imply progression. Whether 'good' or (more commonly) 'bad', however, tritones are always rather special, a disturbance. If they occur in folk music it is usually as intensifications of perfect fifths or fourths.

tumbling strain a phrase invented by the ethnomusicologist Curt Sachs to describe a frequent procedure in primitive musics whereby a vocal phrase starts at a relatively high, strained pitch and then tumbles wildly downwards with an effect of uncontrolled libido. Fourths are the most 'natural' interval to fall through, though some peoples, especially American Indians, tumble through intervals as wide as tenths or even twelfths.

Discography

Rubber Soul	PCS 3075	1965
Revolver	PCS 7009	1966
Sgt. Pepper's Lonely Hearts Club Band	PCS 7027	1967
Magical Mystery Tour	SMAL 2835	1967

   (plus Hello Goodbye; Strawberry Fields Forever;
   Penny Lane; Baby, you're a rich man now; All you need is love)

The Beatles	PCS 7067 and 8	1968

   (the double White Album)

Abbey Road	PCS 7088	1969
Let it Be	PCS 7096	1970

C. The Beatles Soli

PAUL	McCartney	PCS 7102	1970
	Ram	PAS 10003	1971
	Wild Life	PCS 7142	1971
JOHN	John Lennon and Yoko Ono		
AND	Unfinished Music	Zapple 01	1969
YOKO	John Lennon and Yoko Ono		
	Wedding Album	Sapcor 11	1969
	Two Virgins	Sapcor 2/4	1968
	John Lennon and Yoko Ono		
	Live Peace in Toronto	Core 2001	1969–70
	Some time in New York City		
	& Live jam	Apple PCSP 716	1972
JOHN	John Lennon/Plastic Ono Band	PCS 7124	1970
	Imagine	PAS 10004	1971
GEORGE	George Harrison:		
	Wonderwall Music	Sapcor 1	1968
	All Things Must Pass	STCH 1/2/3 639	1970
RINGO	Sentimental Journey	PCS 7101	1970
	Beaucoups of Blues	PAS 10002	1970

Index